Porfiri Ivanov in his natural pose:
in freezing weather in the snow and wearing nothing but trousers.

As a Young Man

PORFIRI IVANOV

Russia's Naturalist Healer

A Biography, Commentary, Description of his
Concepts and Method of Tempering the Body,
and a Translation of Selected Writings
from Russian into English

By:

DANIEL H. SHUBIN

Cover Photograph taken about 1975.

ISBN 978-1-387-55709-7
Copyright 2018
Daniel H. Shubin

February 28, 2018
Email: peacechurch at jps dot net

TABLE OF CONTENTS

Laying in the Snow in his Regular Attire

With Journalists and Visitors

Porfiri with his second wife,
Valentina Leontyevna

During middle age

Out for a stroll in the snow with friends

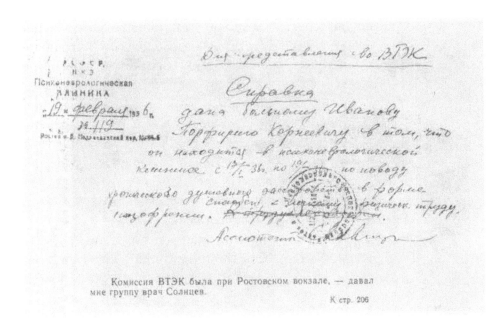

Rostov Psychiatric Clinic notice of psychological illness of
Porfiri Ivanov, dated February 19, 1936

INTRODUCTION

Porfiri Ivanov was an original thinker and unique healer, researcher and practitioner who was able to unite body and cognizance with Nature. His thoughts deal with humanity's stalemate, the doomed situation of the existing relationship between people and Nature, where a person is not supposed to feel that he is a Master over Nature, not to feel that he should have access to its wealth. Porfiri felt that a person should not be dependant on medicines to heal his body of various symptoms and maladies. In place of medicines Porfiri proposed to people that they take responsibility for their own illnesses, that they should discard bad habits, lead an austere and moral life, and utilize air and water and ground to achieve recovery and healing. A person becoming one with Nature will also become one with God.

This was Porfiri's view into the distant future, that once a person grasps the tight mutual relationship of these items a person will not separate from Nature, but will utilize natural products to satisfy his need for survival. By being healthy in body and soul a person will find his happiness and acquire longevity.

A person's morality is indivisible from his attitude toward the surrounding Nature, and it will only disclose its secrets to a person who maintains immaculate feelings and intents. Nature will then gift him with health. As Porfiri stated:

Every person can die, we need to learn how to live.

Detka is Porfiri's method of the restoration of health. This is a simple code consisting of 12 simple statements that are easy for any person to apply to their life. They will allow any person, even the completely weak and ill person, to fortify the strengths of their body as a solid organism and intensify all the reserve strengths as a defensive mechanism against the elements of Nature. As Porfiri felt, by adhering to the concepts of *Detka,* a person can be healed of asthma, diabetes, depression, ischemia, angina, arrhythmia, hypertension, cancer in its early stages, ulcers, tuberculosis, and other diseases. The *Detka* concepts according to Porfiri will also assist in a person's recovery from heart attacks and strokes.

Porfiri practiced his concepts on a number of individuals and claimed that he was able to heal them and restore to them their previous health. He states he possesses an almost miraculous ability to heal them of many illnesses, and which amazed and impressed doctors. This will be noted further in the content of this volume.

The Russian words that Porfiri uses to define his method are Закаливание or закалка. These words have a meaning that is more than treatment or training. The words refer to the metallurgical process of tempering: heating a metal and then quenching it in some cold media in order to harder it. This is Porfiri's best means of describing his treatment: it is a forcing a person into an austere program of intensive training or tempering of his body, hardening his physical faculties, in order to provide it the ability to resist disease and illness, and also to resist the effects of the elements, whether chill or heat. I have used the word *tempering* as the best rendering, although training and treatment also apply.

BIOGRAPHY

Porfiri Korneevich Ivanov was born February 20, 1898, in the village Orekhova, near Lugansk, Ukraine, into a poor miner's family. In addition to Porfiri, his parents had 7 other children and Porfiri was the eldest of the five boys. His initial elementary education was at a parish church school. During childhood and adolescence he had the nickname of Parshek, by which he was referred by friends and relatives. Beginning at 12 years of age he worked as a laborer at a farm that his father rented, and then beginning at 15 years of age he worked in the mines and under difficult working conditions. He had no vocation other than manual labor in the mine, but later he left the mine and worked doing whatever he would be hired to do. Porfiri was a hot-tempered, sharp-witted and intelligent young man. During his adolescence he was delinquent although he had a clear mind and capable of devising pranks, but because of his hard character he was a difficult person with which to get along. His family suffered under the pressure of wealthy persons and as a result Porfiri would find ways of taking vengeance on them for this injustice. With the arrival of Soviet authority he started to work and learn on a more serious basis as he liked the concepts of communism and considered it to be a means of improving the Russian society. (Later he would realize his mistake.)

In 1917, Porfiri was conscripted into the military for World War 1, but he did not see any action as by that time peace was concluded. He did however fight in the Red Army during the

Russian Civil War and with great bravery, for which he received a commendation from the commander of the Red Army.

In early 1918, between World War I and the Civil War, Porfiri married Uliana Feodorevna Gorodovichenko. They were married 55 years to her death in 1973. Porfiri and Uliana had 3 children: a boy Andrei born 1918, a second boy Yakov born 1925, and a daughter, but she died shortly after childbirth.

To provide for his family Porfiri worked at a metallurgical factory, at a shipyard repairing steamships, an expeditor at a manufacturing plant, a safety officer at the Donbass mines, as a supervisor of forest workers, and at other jobs.

In 1922, Porfiri was convicted of not paying patent loyalties, although the crime seems to be fabricated or vague, and he was exiled to Archangelsk Province in the far Russian north, and where he spent 11 months.

In 1928, he moved his family to the city Krasni Sulin, Rostov Province, where he lived until 1971, except for the years 1931-1933, when he lived in the city Armavir, southern Russia. From 1971 to his death he resided in a special guesthouse provided by his disciples in the city Verkhni Kondruchi, Ukraine.

It was here in Krasni Sulin that his capacity and gift for healing materialized. Porfiri wrote in his memoirs:

> In 1933, I encountered my concept and started to occupy myself in treatments in order to utilize all of Nature's available elements to my benefit. I took nothing from the ceiling, nothing that already dealt with national medicine. I listened to lectures on the harmful effects of tobacco and wine. My body refreshed in Nature.

At 35 years of age Porfiri experienced an immense upheaval in his life. He did not just attempt to answer the question as to why a person lives in the world, but was able to grasp, to ascertain, that the meaning of humanity's existence was in a union with Nature through the body, air and ground. It was particularly due to people being accustomed to warmth and a pleasant environment that they started to depart from Nature and as a result become ill.

He let his beard and hair grow, and which annoyed his colleagues at work. Because of some serious altercation with the authorities Porfiri was terminated at his employment in spring 1934, and without the right to work anywhere or anyplace for a term of six months, but this did not devastate him. He decided to dedicate this period of forced unemployment from May to October 1934 to further the development of his concepts of healing.

It was during this period that Porfiri embarked on his famous traversal of the Donbass, wearing only trousers and barefooted. He restrained himself from food and water for long periods, and walked across the Donbass learning and training himself to life with Nature.

When the term of forced absence from work concluded he returned to work, but was immediately terminated. He decided not to return to work at all and started to practice the method of healing that he intuitively conceived. A series of successful treatments resulting in patients' recoveries and restoration to health convinced him of the veracity of his selected route and compelled him to proceed further, this was during the winter of 1934-1935. He then decided to forever stop wearing shoes, and in the spring of 1935, Porfiri stopped wearing clothes forever, except for trousers.

Initially in his life Porfiri was a devout Orthodox Christian, but in time he rejected institutionalized religion, as he concluded that any organized religion contains forces that defeat living principles. However he taught that faith is one of the strongest natural abilities of a person. Concluding that starting a new religion was a mistake, he attempted to utilize faith for the development of cognizance, deciding to complement it with new and unprecedented content. His writings indicate that he had a fluent knowledge of the Gospels and the writings of Apostle Paul.

His strange appearance and no less strange conduct could not but cause him to suffer strange consequences. Sometime in the middle of 1935, Porfiri was taken into custody by the police at the central marketplace of the city Rostov, due to preaching his new convictions. He was assigned to the Rostov Psychiatric Hospital and confined in a cell for violent offenders. There after examination he was diagnosed as having chronic psychological disintegration and schizophrenia. He was transferred to the Rostov Psycho-Neurological Clinic, where he remained until January 1936. The city Rostov medical commission declared Porfiri an invalid of the first class. He was not permitted to work anymore, but instead received a small pension, and he was exempt from military service when World War 2 started.

Porfiri took advantage of the new freedom and so attempted to organize a new group based on his new concepts and defining the principal role as subjectively Nature, rather than specifically some person. Study groups were formed and the following slogan hung in the room each occasion they gathered:

We cannot await for benefits from Nature; we need to just take them from it. This is our task.

In November 1936, Porfiri decided to publicly announce his concepts of natural healing and cold-exposure tempering in Moscow, and no place other that at the Eighth Supreme Soviet Council and where the new Constitution of the USSR was to be reviewed and approved. Included in Porfiri's petition was a paragraph to be included in the constitution regarding rights for the incarcerated and mentally ill.

He showed at Red Square without personal identification, unclothed – except for trousers – and barefoot in the snow and freezing weather. He was immediately taken into custody by the Soviet military police and confined at the infamous Lubyanka prison. While there he spoke with the head of the KGB, Nikolai Yezhov, and who incarcerated him at the Matrosskaya Tishina Prison in Moscow, in isolation. Eventually documents from the Rostov hospital were forwarded to Moscow, and which secured him from worse of a situation and he was released. He was returned to his home as part of a chain-gang of criminals, walking the entire distance to southern Russia, the travel taking 67 days, although the authorities did require him to be clothed due to exposure.

If this was not enough, after his return, and during the winter of 1937, he was arrested by agents of the KGB of the city of Mozdok, the Republic of North Ossetia, as a spy or saboteur, and incarcerated at a local jail. There is no information at to why Porfiri was at Mozdok, 250 miles away from his home and the entire event is baffling. The actual reason for his arrest was that he was bathing in water from a well during weather conditions of 17 degrees below freezing point. As with other situations of this type, Porfiri's faith in Nature helped him withstand the elements, he told people he felt as comfortable as a fish in water. As there was no evidence of any criminal activity on the part of Porfiri, except to have gathered a crowd of spectators that caused the suspicion of the Soviet authorities, after 3 months of incarceration, Porfiri was released.

At this time Porfiri ran 100 miles in 15 hours.

Porfiri was again arrested sometime in 1938, by Soviet agents and confined at the same Rostov Psychiatric Hospital. No information on how long this stay was.

In 1942, with the invasion of Germany into Soviet Russia with World War 2, on their trek toward Stalingrad, and having crossed the Ukraine, Krasni Sulin was occupied by German troops. In autumn 1942, Porfiri encountered the German General Paulus while he was stationed at Krasni Sulin during the German occupation of southern Russia. Some information seems to indicate that German General Friedrich Paulus heard of this unique and extravagant person and gave him a personal order to allow him to leave the occupied territory. The result of the discussion was a security document issued to Porfiri, stating that Porfiri could of be interest to German scientific experiments regarding a person's toleration of the cold. Porfiri was placed on a train scheduled for Berlin. However at Dnipropetrovsk Porfiri was removed from the train and arrested by the Gestapo. Porfiri spent 27 days at the Dnipropetrovsk Gestapo jail in October and November 1942.[1] While there he was buried alive in the snow during the night of November 22, for 13 hours during freezing temperatures, and he survived without any indication of frostbite or other damage. A few days later he was toured around the city for several hours bare-chested on a motorcycle driven by German soldiers, and likewise suffered no damage to his health. He was then released and somehow returned home.

In 1943, Porfiri went to Moscow to Stalin with a proposal of peace with Germany. The occupation of Ukraine and southern Russia by German troops and the suffering of his countrymen motivated Porfiri in its typical manner and in December 1943, he again went to Moscow, now hoping for a personal audience with Marshall Joseph Stalin with suggestions as to how to terminate the war and conclude a successful peace treaty. Finding him at the train station naked in the middle of winter with political demands for Stalin, the military police confined him to the Serbski Psychiatric Institute, a psychiatric hospital well-known for treating dissidents and political prisoners who were declared mentally ill, where he spent 100 days. Afterward Porfiri was confined at some other location and was not released until after the Germans long retreated from Moscow and World War 2 ended, so this would be about 3 years confinement on this occasion.

While at the institute Porfiri had the opportunity to speak with Profession Vvedenski, and asked him to present the petition and convince Stalin of the need for peace. The professor responded that if he was to do this, then he – Vvedenski – would be either shot or himself be confined at that same hospital.

---

[1] There is some doubt to the complete validity of this event, although he was probably arrested and sent to Germany by train with other residents during the German occupation, but then escaped at Dnipro.

Rostov and Krasni Sulin were liberated from the Germans on February 14, 1943. Porfiri's oldest son Andrei died in the battle for the liberation of Rostov.

Porfiri's public displays of his stamina again surfaces in November 1948, so by this time he was back at his home in Krasni Sulin. This next event was his Black Sea Traversal from Tuapse, a town in Krasnodar District on the northwest shore of the Black Sea, and Sochi, about 100 miles south of Tuapse. The event was to celebrate his 50th Birthday and 15 years since the materialization of his natural healing concepts. This event occurred from November 23, to December 5, 1948, and Porfiri, according to his memoirs, stood on the deck of a steamship during the 12 days journey, exposed to the elements and wearing nothing but trousers, and during a Beaufort scale 12 hurricane, meaning wind and rain over 75 miles per hours. During the excursion Porfiri likewise ate and drank nothing and was completely exposed to the hurricane.

(Another account provided by Porfiri is noted later in this volume where he says he walked from Tuapase to Sochi during the storm. Which one is correct is difficult to ascertain, or his recollection may have been a combination of 2 separate events.)

One of Porfiri's greatest feats of enduring the severity of Nature was when during wintertime, with the temperature at 20 degrees below freezing, he stood bare-chested on the front of a steam locomotive during its travel at a high speed over a distance of about 40 miles between 2 train stations in southern Russia.

The next occasion mentioned of Porfiri's altercation with Soviet authorities occurred on February 13, 1951, when he was in Moscow and arrested for violating Statute 58-10 of the Criminal Code: anti-Soviet agitation and propaganda. The place of his latest incarceration was the infamous Taganski Prison in Moscow, but on April 14, by order of the KGB he was assigned to isolation at three psychiatric hospitals and forced to undergo extreme psychiatric treatments. These would have been the typical electrical shock treatments, sleep deprivation, use in medical experiments, anti-psychotic and hallucinatory drugs, and other types of torture and inhumane treatment for which the Soviet Union is known in its procedures in so-called psychiatrics facilities and isolation in prison cells. Porfiri spent almost 4 years in exile and assigned to psychiatric facilities: Leningrad Special Prison Psychiatric Hospital, Chistopol Prison Psychiatric Hospital in Tatarstan Province, and Kazan Special Hospital, spending about a year in each, plus travel by railroad. He was finally released on this occasion on November 29, 1954. Porfiri was labeled a political prisoner and so was deprived of most rights of a Soviet citizen until several years later, in 1971, when he returned to Moscow and applied for official state rehabilitation. The state did not grant Porfiri official rehabilitation status until posthumously on July 7, 2008.

The next 10 years of the Khrushchev regime were relatively quiet for Porfiri, remaining at his Krasni Sulin home and concentrating on his treatments and natural healing techniques with the residents of eastern Ukraine and southern Russia, and writing articles and descriptions of his procedures, and gathering a small group of adherents and disciples.

However on May 23, 1964, Porfiri was again arrested, and this time the charges brought against him were vagrancy and fraud, violation of Section 143 Part 2, of the Ukrainian Criminal Code. This occurred at Bobrinetzk District, Kirovograd Province, central Ukraine. He was held in custody somewhere until departing for Moscow on September 1, 1964, where he was again assigned to the psychiatric ward of the Serbski State Institute. Here he was again diagnosed as mentally ill and now without hope of psychological rehabilitation, however instead of being released Porfiri was transferred to the horrible and inhumane conditions of the Butyrka Prison in Moscow, where he remained until the charges against him were dropped on November 12 (there is no information on the amount of time spent at either Serbski and

Butyrka). However Porfiri was not released, but was again transferred by order of Soviet officials for further treatment at the Kazan Special Hospital of the KGB. He was held here from February 13, 1965 to May 4, 1967, and would have undergone the same treatment as before during his previous internment. Porfiri's next stop was the Novo Rovenetzski Psychiatric Hospital, Rostov Province, where he remained until his case was brought to the Krasni Sulin Court and his release was finally acquired. Porfiri left the hospital with friends and relatives sometime in Spring 1968, finally free again after a 4 year exile.

Disciples and adherents of Porfiri took the effort and constructed a special guesthouse for him in 1971, in the village of Verkhni Kondruchi, Sverdlovsk District, Lugansk Province, Ukraine, about 50 miles west of Krasni Sulin, and this became his new home until he passed away in 1983. Here he was able to again provide his natural healing techniques and treatments to the ill and write his articles.

Porfiri's wife, Uliana Feodorevna Gorodovichenko, died July 3, 1973, falling down from the top of a hay stack. It was very difficult for Porfiri to deal with his wife's death.. He remarried shortly after to Valentina Leontevna Sukharevskaya, a close associate of his for over 20 years and dedicated assistant in his work. His treatments continued successfully and he gathered a large number of disciples and adherents over the next few years.

Again Porfiri wanted to bring his methods of tempering to the attention of Soviet authorities and decided to again travel to Moscow, this time to the XXV Congress of the USSR, which was to be held from November 4, 1975 to March 5, 1976. However KGB agents removed Porfiri from the train during its journey to Moscow shortly after leaving his home, and confined him at the Novoshakhtinsk Psychiatric Hospital, Rostov Province, Russia, near the border with Ukraine. The cruel conditions of the hospital destroyed his health and Porfiri was brought to a point of total physical devastation and psychological ruin, and worse than any of the treatments and torture imposed on him at any of the other psychiatric facilities or prisons. The incessant petitions of his relatives and adherents to have him released were futile, and Porfiri was finally released the day after the closure of the Congress in Moscow, an internment of about 6 months. The Soviet officials wanted to make sure he would not attend. According to the testimony of those who went to retrieve him, his appearance was unbelievably disheveled, wasted and emaciated, as compared to his excellent health of previous years.

Returned to his home at Kondruchi and now under the care of his wife Valentina, Porfiri was gradually able to recover his health, both physically and emotionally. It was three weeks before Porfiri was able to remove himself from his bed and stand on his feet under his own strength. Again he gave the credit for his survival and recovery to his close proximity to Nature.

In one respect all the treatments and tortures of the Soviet psychiatric hospitals and prisons further trained and accustomed Porfiri's physical and mental states for greater tolerance and survival under the extreme elements of Nature. In 1978, with the help of Valentina, Porfiri decided to experiment with prolonged deprivation of food and water. For an entire five months he maintained himself without solid food, and long periods in between he also had no liquids.

But it was not until late 1978, that Porfiri's name was finally circulated into the general public of Soviet Russia regarding himself as a natural healer and his method of tempering. This first public display was a short documentary, and then a short article in a magazine.

Porfiri's adherents decided to have a celebration on his behalf at his guesthouse in Kondruchi, to be held April 25, 1979, and with the secondary purpose of introducing him and his methods of tempering to the general public. But Soviet officials, hearing of the planned event, again interfered. Military police were sent to the village and they set a blockade to his home: no one was allowed within 100 feet of Porfiri's residence and under threat of arrest.

Beginning just prior to the date of the celebration, Porfiri was assigned to house arrest and forbidden to leave for a period of three years. Journalists however later visited Porfiri and wrote of him and more short documentary films were made of the unique man and his methods of natural healing.

The house arrest was lifted only because of an article in the magazine *Flame* (*Ogonyok*), Issue 8, 1982, and which has a distribution throughout the entirety of the Soviet Union, millions of readers. The article was titled, *The Experiment Lasting Half a Century*, and all of his methods and concepts were explained, and which Porfiri also summarized in 7 points. The article caused a flood of letters to Soviet officials demanding a rescission of the interdict, along with a flood of visitors and which was finally granted.

Porfiri's response to the article and flood of letters and visitors was the summary of his concept and method of tempering that he titled *Detka*, and which consisted of 12 points.

Porfiri Korneevich Ivanov died April 10, 1983, at the age of 85 years, at his home in Verkhni Kondruchi. He was buried four days later at the edge of the village cemetery, and opposite the garden where he lived. He had spent 15 years of his life confined in psychiatric hospitals and prisons, and another 3 years under house arrest.

Cartoon with the title: *Path toward Enlightenment*
mimicking Porfiri's method of treatment: bathing in ice water

CONCEPTS AND METHOD OF TEMPERING

When Porfiri reached 35 years of age his life changed. He wrote of himself in the following manner:

> Childhood, adolescence and early adulthood were years of my life spent the same way as any other people. I was not a supernatural person and not to be lauded for any honorable conduct. At one time I would be considered a criminal toward Nature, I plundered it, killed liveliness and happiness, not having regard for anybody, but did what I could for my prosperity. I did what I did so I could live well myself. But then I departed from all of this and started to become friends and friendly with Nature.

What caused this upheaval? When Porfiri was a little over 30 years of age, he writes he was affected by skin cancer that covered one of his hands and arms. No help for him was available and the cancer spread throughout the outside of his body to a final stage where, as with all cancers, he had no choice except to capitulate and slowly die. Then out of despair he decided to speed the terminal process and inflict himself with some other disease. He walked unclothed into the street in freezing cold weather with the intent of getting a chill and then pneumonia, however he did not achieve his desired result. He tried this again, and then on the next occasion he dumped a bucket of ice cold water on himself, but again no results. He repeated this over a course of several days, but instead of the disease spreading he started to acquire strengths he did not previously have, and a desire to live and be jovial. The disease suddenly started to retreat. He noticed the improvement in his health by taking this course of action and so continued his experiment and in the final end he totally recovered.[2]

On April 25, 1933, Porfiri came to the conclusion that the reason for all illnesses and premature deaths was due to humanity's rupture from Nature. According to his concepts the need for food, clothes, and a nice residence lead to a dependant dying life. It is necessary to learn to live independently, to take advantage of the natural conditions of air, water and soil. This concept served as the beginning of a sharp upheaval in Porfiri's life and the start of his 50-year experiment. He started by decreasing the amount of clothes he wore, and then after two years, lived year round in solely trousers and barefooted. April 25 is celebrated by Porfiri's followers as the Anniversary Day of the birth of his concepts of living in accord with Nature.

This event had an immense impact on him. Earlier Porfiri was perplexed with the question as to why a person is subject to illness and death, regardless of the many comforts of life that surround him. And now the thought sprouted in his mind, "Why is this? Because a person hides himself, secludes himself, from Nature that wants to provide him health and recovery!" No began his searches to find the answer to that question, "Perhaps some secret is hidden in Nature and in an individual." He started his experimental tempering while drawing close to Nature. He gradually denied himself those items that caused Nature to distance itself from him. Initially he removed his hat while walking in freezing weather and in the wind. He wanted to verify if he was on the proper route, and if other people just as himself could also receive the same results of recover as he did. So he then started to propose to people who were suffering from diverse

---

[2] Although Porfiri states this was skin cancer, as there was no official medical diagnosis, the disease can be debated, and could just as well be some other skin condition, such as psoriasis.

maladies to do what he did. Yes, this did happen and they recovered their health, meaning that his tempering was effective. But not everyone had this same amount of boldness and enthusiasm to proceed on their own. Then he decided to experiment, whether he had the ability to heal these people using the same strengths that he received from Nature and get the same results from the tempering.

In 1934, Porfiri started to treat himself. He had no teacher, no one of whom to ask advice, where to start, what he needed to know, and no books were available. He sacrificed his body to find and so be able to provide to people the means and route of tempering for them to gain their health while in this struggle against Nature, in other words, Porfiri used himself as the experiment. On April 25, 1934,[3] he stopped wearing a hat, regardless of weather conditions, and he actually felt better and ceased to get headaches. During the winter of 1934-1935, the cold, even freezing weather, did not harm him at all, and so he decided to increase his exposure, and started to wander outdoors at nights without a shirt and remain this way for first 10 minutes, then 15 and then 30 minutes. Beginning that summer of 1935, he discarded all his clothes except trousers and shoes, and traversed the steppes and forests of the Donbass. He studies the effects of Nature on his body and so utilized this to develop strength. It was during autumn of 1935, he returned to work, but did not discard his concepts of the new method of tempering. It was this winter that he first walked the streets without shoes, initially for a course of two hours barefoot in the snow, and even at the ridicule of those who encountered him and who almost forced him to put on some shoes. This was the first occasion of him walking in the snow barefoot and which had no harmful effects on him.

---

[3] Although the Russian text states 1934, the same date is used in 1933, for a similar event, mentioned above. Over the course of time, somehow the 2 years seem to be interchanged.

This entire period he sought in Nature a confirmation of the veracity of his actions, and he received this when soon after by using his tempering he was able to heal a woman who did not walk for 17 years. So did his experiment proceed: he aspired to become closer to Nature. So he stopped wearing a hat, then gradually not wearing shoes, and then a shirt, until all he wore were trousers. He spent more time in Nature. His health was fortified and he proceeded to encounter all the elements of Nature, whichever they might be, and he did not hide from any but walked right into Nature with assurance and love and without fear. Nature like an intelligent and living entity provided him strengths and as though taught him, ascertaining his sincerity and showing him his errors, as he wrote about himself:

> I learned about all that resides in a person and in Nature that causes weakness and ruins, and all that fortifies and develops, and I found access and knowledge, and a method to develop and utilize it for myself and each person.

As a result he was able to achieve what he sought, and so was able to spend a week in the steppes in freezing weather exposed to the environment and without shoes and not get sick. He trained himself with the help of cognizance and volition to control his body and psyche, so not to allow illness, weakness, lethargy, to affect him. He learned how to survive without food and water for prolonged periods of time and without it doing any harm to him. The longest interval in his experiments pertaining to survival without food was for 108 days, but according to Porfiri, he still did not reach the limit of his capability.

It was about this time that Porfiri started to propagate his method of remedy and tempering to any person he would encounter and so helped the sick and the weak to defeat their illnesses and rise from their beds. He tested the useful qualities of Nature that he discovered on willing people and during the healing interval he would observe them and control their progress.

As he said about this in his *History and Method of my Tempering*, sent to scholars and doctors in 1951:

> This is not a normal tempering of the body as an organism against cold and chill, but a stimulation, development and conscious control using inner strengths and capacities of the nervous system.

Gradually Porfiri developed and formulated his set of rules of tempering and assigned it the appellation of *Detka*, meaning child, as this is how he dealt with every person to whom he applied his tempering – as his child. This set of rules was likewise sent to the Kremlin, to then ruler of Soviet Russia, L.I. Brezhnev. Up to this time Porfiri transmitted the rules of his tempering orally. The attitude of the authorities toward him, of course, was very cautious. In every manner possible they would attempt to interfere with him and disrupt him. Of the 85 years of his life, a total of 15 years were spent in prisons and psychiatric hospitals, where they tortured him and brought him almost to a point beyond his toleration of physical abuse and then released him and sent him home to literally die. However once returning home he gradually recovered from his ordeals and restored his health, again exposing his body to Nature to gain its strengths.

What is also principal is that in this communion with Nature his cognizance participated along with his body. His mode of thinking changed almost completely. He acknowledged his previous vices and defeated them, meaning, he subjected them to his volition. The matter is that almost nothing can be achieved in Nature, much less health, if the person retains moral vices or malevolent emotions and does not attempt to subdue them. Nature as if senses them residing in a person, and so a person who maintains vices or addictions will soon succumb to cold weather or starve without food within a short interval. But Nature will unveil itself to a person who possesses positive and immaculate feelings and thoughts, will help him endure the elements, and Nature will entrust its strengths to him as though it is willing to work with the person.

His love and patience toward people was immeasurable. He endured so many insults and offenses from them beginning right when he first came to the notion of this natural tempering and over the next 50 years until his death, and he was still maligned even after his death. But this did not stop him all those decades and did not embitter him, and he did not change his stance toward Nature's cooperation with a person's health and continued to help any person who was willing to ask him for his tempering and he gave all he possible could in the process. His soul was in pain for the destitute, underprivileged and sick, and the only way for him to remove this pain was to help them recover. Porfiri seemed to have a penetrating vision to look right through a person at first sight already knowing why this person came to him and the tempering he needs. He aspired to stimulate each person's conscious, help the person defeat pride and conceit, and fear and contempt, distrust of people, motivate love in them. And to the extent they wanted to change and improve their lives, to this extent his tempering was successful. He hid nothing from people and carefully detailed every segment of his tempering or experiment as he applied it to a person, and as the person applied it to himself, for him to understand the affect of Nature in healing.

Porfiri likewise presented his finding to the authorities. And if they did not include him or support him in accomplishing his intents he did not cause them trouble or take vengeance, as one of his life-long principles was, "Implement yours and do not interfere with others," also, "Nature pertains to all of us, to our wants." Porfiri did not attempt to as if jump over the heads of Soviet doctors or scholars or to force his concepts on others. To him, the utilization of force or violence, and even revolution, does not accomplish anything (and which he realized later in his life with regard to the Russian Revolution), and instead a person needs to live evolutionary, to gradually implement changes relative to the growth of people's cognizance and the changes in environment and the effects of Nature. We need to know that his goal did not just consist in each person being healthy on his own, not to feel pain, and to live happily, but also first of all to change the current of people's cognizance, their manner of life, their attitude toward Nature and themselves. Porfiri felt that our primordial and initial form of life and our attitude toward Nature leads humanity and each distinct person toward stagnation, to causing our own ruin. This becomes all the more apparent right now with our connection with the appearance of serious global problems for humanity, the evidence indicating that our planet is right now exhausting and violating the ecological balance. Humanity's activities presently threaten the annihilation of the planet and us along with it. The human is uneducated in this respect and has no ability to view what occurs on the entirety of this planet and in humanity due to its large scale. He lives in his withdrawn little world with his egoistic interest, looking at everything from the point of view of what will be to his advantage, his benefit, not thinking about the consequences of his actions. Just a little while longer and all can terminate in a catastrophe, the extravagant human race with all of its accomplishments, this master of Nature and his own destiny, will cease to exist and will vanish without a trace.

The human does not utilize half his capabilities, and he has the capacity to build a life that is prosperous, and one that will not reach some sorrowful conclusion.

Porfiri began using the nickname of Parshek that he received as a child in later years to refer to himself as a divine miracle healer and special emissary of God. According to his statements, "I am the conqueror of Nature, God for the Earth. I arrived to Earth for the salvation of life." In this regard Parshek is also the mediator through whom the miracle working power of Nature is bestowed on people. Through Parshek, Nature "has gifted happiness to people and introduced health for them and forever." Parshek is a key figure in the realization of the consummate goal of humanity.

In this manner, Parshek felt the spirit within him had merged with the divine Spirit and he became the materialization of the divine Spirit, and viewed his mission as the responsibility of introducing this to others, so they could also attain this state. So Porfiri felt he could speak in the first person although it was the divine Spirit in him who was speaking, as he stated, "All of you people through Me as God will attain immortality and cease to die. You will live eternally as a result of your glory."

Porfiri has a unique concept of the application of deity. He introduces attempts to provide a parallel between the Christian teaching of the Trinity and the coming Kingdom of God with his personal system: God the Father materializes as deified Nature. Parshek as the victor over Nature applies to himself the role of Jesus Christ and is the incarnation of the Holy Spirit. The Chuvinski Hill[4] assumes the roll of the place for the coming transformation of humanity, where a person will attain immortality. All of these three elements: Nature – Parshek – Chuvinski Hill, are mutually tied and now replace the divine three: God – Jesus – Kingdom.

God is inherent in Nature and subject to it. Nature becomes as though a new hypostasis of god and by blending with it the person acquires salvation. The entire system of Porfiri's religious views is pervaded with the idea of his special messianic mission.

In the same vein Parshek has introduced the belief of the Third Covenant or the Covenant of the Holy Spirit or the Second Arrival of Jesus Christ. Based on this premise Ivanovtzi consider Porfiri to be the returned Jesus Christ and in whom the Holy Spirit is now incarnated. In a similar application, Porfiri writes that the Father and Son fulfilled their purpose in the past, while the Third, the Holy Spirit, has its role in the present or near future. The key role is assigned to the Holy Spirit in the realization of the new person, but it is not the Holy Spirit of the Gospels, but some kind of cosmic energy. The appearance of the

---

[4] Mentioned in Profiri's article *The Teacher*, at the end of this volume.

Spirit will signify the beginning of evolutionary history of humanity.

What is worth also noting is Porfiri's attitude that God does not reside in heaven, but here on Earth, in people who were able to attain this victory over themselves.

Even then Porfiri discusses sin and the need for a person's renovation. He speaks of the parable of the Prodigal Son and quotes many passages from the New Testament. Based on his writings, Porfiri had a fluent knowledge of the New Testament and also a deep faith in God.

Porfiri described himself in the following terms, although seeming to many to be unorthodox:

> All are awaiting the second arrival: God will appear from the clouds in golden attire and in a gold crown. But he ascended from a prison and hospital, and he possessed no beauty.
>
> So Parshek arrived on Earth, the conqueror of Nature, the Teacher of the nation, God for the Earth. With his unprotected body, being naked and barefooted, he blazed a new unprecedented route into Nature. The Lord materialized to display Himself in the flesh, as this is stated in the books of the ancestors.[5] Indeed this actually occurred, the strength of the Omnipotent made its residence in this flesh, and the Teacher was born from the Potency of Nature. Just as it gave birth to the human, so did it give birth to the Teacher. And then in this flesh it planted His Spirit, the sole one for the Universe and for this matter.

The messiah has already arrived, who is Parshek, the second arrival of Jesus and God for the Earth. He refers to himself also as

---

[5] Referring to the Bible

The Teacher sent to unveil the manner a person can blend with Nature.

Porfiri passed on to another world in 1983, leaving behind his concepts recorded in notebooks containing over 250 pages of information, his *Detka* system of tempering, and an abundant number of letters to authorities, scholars and doctors. Porfiri's system of healing has thousands of adherents who aspire to unite with Nature as a means of wellness, they call themselves Ivanovtzi. Porfiri left behind a humble petition to people:

I ask, I beseech all people: Stand and take your place in Nature. Your spot is not occupied by anyone else and cannot be purchased for money, but it is only through your individual efforts and exertion will Nature be utilized to your benefit, so life will be easier and better for you.

INTERESTING FACTS

Over the years of 1933-1983, Porfiri was able to compose 300 notebooks and diaries of text regarding himself, his experiences and his tempering, as well as a considerable amount of poetry, several hundred pages, and letters he sent and received. They were distributed clandestinely by his followers over the years through photocopies.

Scholars studying Ivanov claim to have found elements of neo-paganism and neo-Christianity embedded in his concepts, as well as similarities with traditional Taoist, Hindu and Buddhist concepts scattered. However an objective analysis of both his writings as well as his education and experiences testify that Porfiri's concepts have a Russian derivation and he was not affected by any influences from Oriental traditions or religions, and any similarities are solely accidental or superficial.

Russia does have a group of adherents of Porfiri's concepts and methods of tempering, and who are called Ivanovtzi. They are for the most part divided into two categories: one holds to his basic methods of tempering pertaining to the health of the body as an organism; the other inclines toward a religious-mystic interpretation of his teachings. Some of these adherents have gone to the extent of almost deifying Porfiri, as being the incarnation of the morals ideals of Christianity. Contemporary researches view the Ivanovtzi as a new religious movement in Russia, although their number is relatively small and their influence is more of a novelty than one to be taken seriously. Russians who are inclined toward Porfiri's methods of tempering probably only number a few hundred, or thousand at most, and they are limited to an occasional bath in the icy waters of Russia or a stroll in freezing weather through the fields and villages.

Out for a stroll in public

SELECTED ARTICLES OF

PORFIRI IVANOV

TRANSLATED FROM THE ORIGINAL RUSSIAN INTO ENGLISH

Practicing his healing technique on a client

THE HISTORY AND METHOD OF MY TEMPERING

1. WHY I BECAME AN INNOVATOR

I became an innovator not because I wanted to acquire financial gain or credit from people.

Those people who want to become innovators only for the sake of financial gain and credit are not innovators in any sense of the word, but are bad people, deceivers, because their principal purpose is not truth, but credit and money.

I am not at all one of these people. On the contrary, in my work and searches, I have declined money and luxury in my life. On the contrary I have consciously proceeded to become a sacrifice and joke, even denying myself what other people normally have.

I became an innovator because from early childhood I sensed in myself the strength and aspiration to accomplish something special, something useful to people, although I did not initially know what this particularly was. I simply knew one thing at the beginning: that I needed to help all the destitute and suffering people, and that this help could be found but needed to be sought in something that was new, and not in the old or mundane. All my life I aspired to leave behind the old and proceed to the new and unprecedented. I am an innovator because Nature created me to be this way and provided me a life to do this. I am a innovator because I was born in an old life, among the needs and sicknesses of a destitute and laboring nation, because I read Karl Marx's *Capital*, and realized that laboring people must arise and become masters of their World and all of Nature. This is the reason I participated with others in the revolution, and this is why later I separated from all of them and started to depart from the people of the past, from lethargic people, those who were lazy in regard to the future. I started to sacrifice myself in order to work for the future, in order to penetrate into it even if alone, to acquire its wealth, to take these abundant harvests available and provide it to poor and suffering people and present to them the Route to this wealth.

2. WHEN AND WHAT BROUGHT ME TO THE CONCEPT OF THIS TEMPERING?

From early childhood I was very impressionable and curious of all of Nature, of all that surrounded life. I had compassion for people to the awesome extent of weeping on their behalf, especially the poor. I noticed how people around me were in pain, suffering and dying prematurely and because they did not have the means or the capacity of withstanding the effects of Nature, its horrifying powers of cold and illness.

When I was seven years of age my grandfather right in front of my eyes fell and died due to a whirlwind in the field. Along with the sorrow and fear the kernel of this Concept of the absolute necessity of comprehending Nature and the ability for a person to defend himself from it was born and flared in me. What especially did not allow me to forget about it and motivated this kernel within me was the illness and death of so many people during the cholera epidemic in the year 1913, and which I still continued to see surrounding myself in my life. But a field and gardener for this kernel was still lacking. I felt within myself the strength to become a hero for my nation, but I was deficient in finding this spot or a course of education applying to it. I did not know how to apply my strengths on behalf of people so they could deal with the effects of Nature.

So life then instructed me and I did myself. My Concept did not just sprout, but it was unveiled within me clearly as a result of a practical application of my life.

During the winter of year 1933, I saw one man who was walking without a hat and he did not fear the frost, chilling or illness. All of a sudden a thought enlightened me, that it is possible for a trained person to not fear Nature. This person possessed the strength to withstand Nature, and so I could also, and every other person, have these strengths and could develop them further. This thought knocked at my head day and night to enter it, and so once in 1934,[6] when I was sitting in the evening behind a book and went into a trance for a moment due to exhaustion, I saw in a dream a handsome appearance of a man who was boldly strolling through the snow undressed. This pictured caused me to awaken with excitement and this picture became an example and goal for me.

Later that year another endeavor still clandestinely residing deep in my soul unveiled itself in a turbulent and brilliant dream. This dream was the following: I saw myself having crawled to the top and edge of a large haystack that was standing on a virgin field, one never plowed, and the haystack consisted of layers of clean sheaves of wheat. All of a sudden the haystack started to rise at the other end and the sheaves of wheat started to collapse on me from every side, but I was not crushed when it tipped over me. At the conclusion I noticed I was at the very pinnacle of an entire mountain of expensive sheaves of different grains. I understood this dream in the following manner: The haystack is Nature, while its sheaves are its conditions and strengths and they are its wealth, and if I was to boldly climb into Nature it will collapse on me with all of its conditions and strengths. But because they are its strength I will not be crushed underneath it,

---

[6] The date should be 1933. Another transposition of dates by Porfiri.

but on the contrary will rise to the very summit of a complete and immense pile of this wealth of Nature, as its master.

As a result of this in 1934, the Concept and Bold Decision to discover and develop this strengths within myself matured. I was not to fear Nature but proceed into Nature in order to acquire its wealth, its conditions and strengths, so all of this within me would proceed for the benefit of the nation, and not for its harm or terror; for a person not to fear Nature, for a person not to suffer due to Nature, or be subdued by it, as a result of the weakness of his body, but that he would become master of his body and all of Nature. I decided to train and exercise my body in a manner that it would not be harmed by Nature, but would be utilized to a benefit, to blaze this trail to the riches of Nature on behalf of our nation and each person.

3. When and How I Started my Tempering

I started my tempering in the year 1934, when living in the city Armavir,[7] during my spare time from work at the Armavir Forestry Collective Union.

I had no one to teach me, and no one to even ask for some advice as to how to start and what to do, and no books on this subject were available.

I only had a goal and a desire, and whatever it is that I had to do to achieve this. From childhood I distinguished myself by having this bold and despairing character pertaining to any endeavor. I threw my body as a sacrifice in order to find and transmit to people the Means and Route of Tempering and Health for their struggle against Nature.

---

[7] A city in Krasnodar region, Russia, on the Kuban River, about 50 miles east of Krasnodar.

4. THE ROUTE AND STAGES OF MY TEMPERING

On April 25, 1934, I removed my hat for ever and no matter what the weather, cold or rain, I decided not to wear it and did not, regardless of the cold and rain with wind. Walking with an uncovered head I did not just not catch a cold or acquire headaches, but on the contrary I started to actually feel better, especially in the rain and fog. My head really became clearer and I felt a gush of health and strength. For this reason I decided to not wear a hat even during winter, and during the winter of 1934-35, I traversed the entire season without a hat. Noticing such successes, that even frost does not harm my uncovered head, but adds health, fortitude and strength to it, this winter I decided to expand my curriculum of tempering and started to attempt walking into freezing weather at nights without a shirt, but I did wear felt-lined boots and pants. Initially in the frost without a shirt it was 10 minutes, then 15, then 30, and as a result I felt so well and energetic, just like after a cold shower. I then went into public without a shirt during the entire final month of that winter.

In December 1934, I moved my residence from Armavir to a new house in Krasni Sulin.[8] For a short interval I interrupted my involvement in this tempering so not to annoy relatives and friends with my unusual behavior, so they would not count me to be insane. I lived and worked as did all others, but this did not satisfy me. Then in May 1935, when some people felt that I was acting like a priest, I was terminated from my employment and was not allowed to return to work for six months. So I decided to again relocate and devote myself entirely to my innovative venture. Having discarded all my clothing except for my trousers, during the summer of 1935, I traveled the steppes and forests of

---

[8] Krasni Sulin is the administrative center of Krasnosulinski District in Rostov Province, Russia. It is about 300 miles north of Armavir.

the Donbass,[9] learning on my own, taking advantage of the effects of the various conditions and forces on Nature on my body as a organism: air, wind, rain, sun, the morning and evening dawns, the electrical atmosphere during storms, and I ascertained its effect on me, and so I developed strengths and new capabilities of my body as an organism, and especially pertaining to the alimentary and nervous systems, as master of my entire entity.

It was at this time that I started to preach my method of tempering and wellness to any person I would encounter and so helped the sick and weak to overcome their illnesses and rise from their cots.

During this summer season I strengthened my health and developed the defensive capacities of my body as an organism to such a degree that I achieved the total control of my body and learned to utilize diverse strengths and conditions of Nature to my benefit. Autumn of 1935, ended the six months of my forced unemployment, and so in order to provide for my family I returned home, put my clothes back on and reentered the work force, except that I did not wear a hat.

Over the course of one month, while I was getting used to the new employment assigned me, I was not engaged in my tempering but only tested my strengths and methods by helping the sick. But during this entire time I did not cease to think as to what I had to do to achieve my goal, to complete my tempering and to its terminal point, for my body to not fear winter and snow. I decided to gradually proceed on this course rather than forcing it to immediately materialize.

My successful healing of many and various illnesses indicated to me that I already possessed extraordinary strengths and capability to manage my body and even the bodies of other people by using these concealed powers. This encouraged me to achieve the essential goal of my tempering.

---

[9] The Donetsk Basin, a region in eastern Ukraine, and bordering the Rostov Province. The central forest is about 50 miles west of Krasni Sulin.

At the beginning of December 1935, Bondaronko, an officer who was a friend of mine and who worked as a guard at the Ovechkino train station,[10] knowing that I was healing the ill, asked me to help his ill mother who had not walked on her feet in 17 years. So far I had not the opportunity to deal with such a serious crippling illness but decided to acquire a victory. I decided that if I had the strength to deal and get the better of this crippling disease, then that winter I would walk in the snow barefooted.

I took upon myself the responsibility to heal this crippled woman who had not walked in 17 years, and so by the second day of my tempering I was easily able to get her to walk about her room, and within a week she started to walk normally as did any other person. As a result of this, that winter – in January 1936 – it was 12 degrees below freezing in the steppes. So I removed my boots and for the course of an hour I walked barefooted in the snow. I did not catch a chill or get sick in any manner, on the contrary, I received this excellent sensation in my feet. The amazement, misunderstanding and ridicule of people forced me to put my boots back on, but as a result the incident assured me that I could walk barefooted in the snow without being harmed, and from this time forward I walked barefooted if I so wanted during summer and winter in any weather condition.

These efforts of mine were not systematic, but at the beginning of May 1936, when I was working at the Tikhoretsk region as a fully-authorized supervisor in central scheduling at the Russian Transport Office, it was because of my involvement in my treatment and help of the ill that I was eventually terminated and now permanently. I then discarded all of my clothing except my trousers and decided to finally, and to reaching my goal, dedicate my total self to the development of my method of treatment and possession of the strengths of Nature and the body as a whole organism. From this time on I never again wore a hat

---

[10] In the Bykovsky District, Volgograd Province, east of Rostov Province.

or shoes except in those circumstances when I was in a city or in some village where I was compelled to wear them because of the residents, but this was only temporary.

This means that beginning in 1936 and for the course of the next 16 years[11] I could walk and did walk during summer and winter without clothing, and more and more learned about myself and Nature and expanded my utilization of Their strengths and conditions for this treatment, to ward off illness and overcome illnesses. Over this period not once did I ever catch a cold or get sick.

5. THE RESULTS AND ACHIEVEMENT OF MY TEMPERING

Regardless of people of science and scholarship did not help me, but just interfered with me the entire time, and hindered and interrupted my work, I proceeded with it studying it without teachers and theory. Due to my treatment I achieved the following results with my body. Achievement in developing my volition and the conscious control of my body in life.

Over the course of one year, 1934, I modified my life and forever denied myself all of the harmful and bad habits of my entire earlier life: drinking alcoholic beverages, smoking, unrestrained verbosity and profanity, fighting, gambling and especially playing cards, egoism, bullying, impoliteness toward people, dishonesty, artificial piety, promiscuity, and a dissolute life in general, and more. All of my feelings, wants and passions I subjected to my will and cognizance.

I took control of my volition, the cognizance of my physical ability, and the reserved strengths of my body as an organism.

I trained myself to be able to stand on my feet for several days at a time without getting tired; I avoided sleep also for several days at a time and also without getting tired; I avoided food over

---

[11] This article was written in 1951.

the course of 16 days without a problem, and I did not lose my strength, and once even longer as a result of necessity; I avoided water and other beverages for the same length of time; I submerged myself under water and not breathing for three hours straight; I withheld the natural disposal of the body's wastes without difficulty for several days and without any harmful side effects; I developed the capacity to run fast and for long distances without exhaustion and as exercise, for example in 1937, I ran from Voroshilovgrad[12] to Stalino,[13] and half the distance through the fields, a total of 100 miles in 15 hours. My goal was not to establish some kind of record, but only to develop my breathing and the control of my willpower, and to exercise my nervous system, and etc.

I trained myself to be unaffected by chill or illness, but reoriented it toward benefiting my body to be able to tolerate the deleterious external effects of the conditions of Nature: not to fear the sun, cold, dampness, wind and rain, to walk without clothing and shoes at any time of the year. Some of what I achieved are the following:

1. The hottest summertime heat, the southern sun, did not harm me or even give me a sunburn;
2. I walked during the winter without clothes or shoes at a temperature of 46 degrees below freezing and in the snow;
3. The Germans were able to train their personnel to tolerate snow only up to half-an-hour, but when they buried me [in the snow], steam exuded from my body due to its heat;
4. I can bathe during winter weather in the sea or in a river, remaining unaffected by the season;
5. After a stay in a steam room, while sweaty and wet, I walk home without clothes in the frost and snow barefooted, and I like it even better when I flounder in the snow;

---

[12] Today known as Lugansk, a city in eastern Ukraine.
[13] Today known as Donetsk, a city in central eastern Ukraine.

6. During wintertime, with temperatures 20 degrees below freezing, to test my potential I stood bare-chested on the front of a steam locomotive during its travel at a high speed from Gluboki station[14] to Millerovo station.[15]

7. I stood exposed bare-chested to a storm on a steamship in the middle of autumn, during a heavy rain and wind, and I did not suffer any chill.

8. I walked through Autumn and Spring rains, impassible roads, fog, puddles, dampness of every sort, barefooted and bare-chested and without any affect on myself, but on the contrary I acquired a benefit from this and far more than from sitting in a warm apartment on quiet days.

9. Even if I accidentally was affected by frostbite with blisters on my legs, I defrosted myself from the cold and eventually recovered and without any trace of harm within a few hours.

10. The final pinnacle of the achievement of my endeavor due to this tempering of my body as a whole organism was the development of such defensive strengths and the ability to subject them to my will, and which permitted me to not only endure any conditions whatsoever without harm imposed on me, but right from the onset to defeat any possible illnesses, and not just with me but also in other people.

Utilizing this capability of mine and latent strengths, and those also installed in each person, I easily achieved a disruption of the course of even the most serious and long-term illnesses, and where the regular medical treatments of doctors were of no help to these people. Not occupying myself with special medical practices, and since they were not allowed me anyway, I only utilized my experience at the request of those ill and suffering people whom I would encounter and whom no one else could help. I healed chronic malaria, paralysis, rheumatism, serious tuberculosis,

---

[14] Glubokaya Railroad station, in Gluboki, Kamenski county, Rostov province.
[15] Millerovo Railroad station, north of Gluboki, about 40 miles.

stomach ulcers, duodenum ulcers, stomach cancer, asthma, dysentery, eczema, heart disease, angina, grippe, headaches, appendicitis, venereal disease, night blindness, trachoma, and other diseases.

Over the entirety of the 16 years of my tempering, not once was I ill.[16] The facts and the achievement of my tempering were verified by German professors and generals during the era of World War II, when I fell into their hands during their occupation of the Donbass. But I did not disclose anything to them, and did not say anything about my treatments. These facts are also well known even in the Rostov State Medical Institute. I discussed and proved this to professors N.N. Kurchakov and A.B. Korgan.[17] Many other witnesses other than them can confirm the success of my treatments, and I can at any time repeat them and do even more.

6. MY METHOD OF TEMPERING

In my personal practice, I did not receive all of the achievements of my tempering so much due to the gradual procedure and special system, as much as because since birth I possessed special strengths and capabilities and approaches and which were all tangible, and so I took the risk to unveil and utilize them. As a result I immediately received great results. But this does not mean that I am the only one who can do this, and that this is impossible for anyone else to accomplish, or that no one else should do the same.

On the contrary, this is possible and necessary for each person because such strengths and capabilities are confined in a latent state in the body of each person, except that he does not know

---

[16] This article was written in 1951, 16 years after the start of Porfiri's tempering.
[17] Aleksander Borisovich Kogan, 1912-1999, a neuro-physiologist. No information on Kurchakov.

about them and cannot know them, but can control them should he want to.

I allowed them to be displayed, controlled them, learned all about what it is inside a person and in Nature that causes weakness and ruins, and all that promotes strength and development, and I found the means, knowledge and methods to develop and guide them on my behalf and for the benefit of each person.

I tested all of these strengths and capabilities on an immense number of situations and they were all healed of their illness. Displaying and utilizing all of this I achieved unseen results: it was my tempering in the fight against illness in Nature and in each person, and even about the ill who spent years in bed in the most helpless and weak states. Many people, as a result of their talent and healthy conditions of life, possess these strengths and capabilities more than I do, but they are just not aware of it.

My method of tempering provides not only the regular tempering of the body as an organism against cold and chills, but includes the stimulation and development of all inner defensive strengths of the mechanism of the body, due to which a person can endure any unpleasant circumstances without being harmed and even utilizing the situation to their benefit. It can also cure any illness, including cancerous illness whose cause or source is still not completely known.

What is principal in my method is the unusual gradual adaptation of the body as an organism to unpleasant external conditions. It is not a system of external physical exercises and its effect on the body, and which materializes as prolonged and little effective, but it is a psycho-technical means of stimulation, development and conscious motivation of inner strengths and capabilities of the nervous system, and especially its reserve strengths and mechanical means of warmth and immunity.

The most principal of all of these psycho-technical means of tempering according to my method, and which has the most important significance, is the means of direct stimulation and inclusion of all of these strengths and mechanisms in their mutual cooperation. All of them are prepared and can operate in each person, except that they are located in a deep latent and dormant state, not yet disclosed to the person and not subjected to his volition and cognizance.

Further tempering consists in bringing into order these mechanisms, those that are weakened and dispersed as a result of ignorance and a bad manner of life, and then the subjection of these mechanisms to our cognizance and volition through systematic exercises and in the development of strength and change by a route of utilizing the various means, conditions and strengths of Nature, and likewise the disclosure of the means to utilize new and still unknown, latent strengths of our body and Nature.

The length of the term for a complete course of tempering is one year, but the initial decisive success in tempering can be reached within 30 hours and even almost immediately.

My method of tempering is applicable to each person what wants to receive and possess health for himself that is undefeatable. However for one person it may be acquired almost immediately, while for another it may be a half-year of effort, while for another it may take a year.

7. CONDITIONS AND PROGRAM FOR TEMPERING ACCORDING TO MY
    METHOD

Since for the person who undertakes my method of tempering a stimulation and inclusion of all of these latent defensive strengths and capabilities surfaces in the body as the person's organism, and which a person on his own volition cannot motivate and direct any of this, it is only I who disclosed this and can do this for myself and others, then the tempering according to my method can be successful only through the direct assistance of myself and my guidance, or through the person whom I have trained.

The course for the immediate success in tempering can be successful, but not for every person, and not for any situation, and not under any circumstances. In order for this course to be successful the following is necessary:

7.1. The person at that specific moment cannot be physically or psychologically ill, intoxicated or under the influence of any toxic substance.

7.2. It is necessary for the person to be aware of the possibilities of what this tempering can accomplish, he needs to know that he maintains latent strengths that can materialize, and needs to believe that he can stimulate them, that I – Ivanov – or someone else from among my disciples can stimulate them, and he needs to passionately want this and aspire to this himself.

7.3. It is necessary for this person to have resoluteness and determination of volition for the sake of receiving such tempering. From this moment and forward he must deny himself wine, hard liquor, tobacco, and all other narcotics and also sexual excess.

7.4. It is necessary for a person to take this route without any secret reservations from his side or doubts within himself.

7.5. Meanwhile a person must at this moment locate himself right next to me and be ready, and without any fear or doubt, to accomplish all that I will say to him.

7.6. All that remains and what is principal depends also on me.

7.7. First of all I take him by the right hand with my right hand and squeeze my left cheek to his left cheek and lean my chest against his chest in a posture so that my heart is directly opposite to his heart. Meanwhile I voice my desire for him and say to him, "I want you to absorb my personal health, while your illness I absorb into myself." What he should respond to me is not important, but he must transfer his illness to me and he must transfer my health into him.

7.8.   I will ask the person to think about me, and I will think about him. In this manner we establish a mutual contact that must never in the future be disrupted.

7.9.   By means of the transfer of my strength of volition emanating like invisible radio waves, I take my thoughts and throw them initially very high, into the depths of the universe, and then retract them and move them into the depths of the water and ground, and then transfer them to all the offended entities living in Nature and then into the Person. I penetrate into his body with my inner vision and touch, beginning from the brain in his head and to the tips of his toes and the hands and heart and lungs and all the other organs, except the stomach, and some others I need not mention.

7.10. Penetrating into the body of the person with my inner vision and touch, and especially into the nervous system in his head, as though with an electrical shock, I stimulate and install into it these latent strengths and defensive capabilities.

7.11. After all of this is finished I release his hand and ask him – if we are sitting inside a room – for him to go outside and get some fresh air, but if we are already in fresh air then we just sit where we are, raise our face upward, inhale and exhale deeply three times.

7.12. The person, after doing all of this, can boldly proceed toward any conditions and not be harmed.

7.13. Later he must daily, in order to repel any possible infections, perform this three-time inhale and exhale, in the morning and in the evening, and wash his feet with cold water.

Note: After such a short course of a person's tempering, if he appears conducive to perform all of this and honestly and austerely accomplishes all of my directives and his promises, and will observe and develop the tempering as he receives it and even more his entire life, all will be well. Even in the situation if the tempering occurs during summer, he can boldly proceed the following winter in any weather conditions, and so he will not only not lose his health, but will more and more develop and strengthen his defensive mechanisms and the capabilities of his body.

Flaws in the method of immediate tempering appear when the person is not suitable for the complete tempering at any moment and only starts the process.

People who are older and have distempered health and strength and do not possess firm belief and volition, can receive tempering only as the result of a strict and special regimen and more of a prolonged effort on themselves with my help and under my guidance.

The 30-hour course of tempering begins with the preliminary and then proceeds further:

7.14.   The person wanting tempering and to receive his health, once discovering that he can do this using my method and only with my help, turns to me with his request to do this and with firm resolution and promise, with no reservations or doubts, must be willing to perform the entire process to the end in the manner I will direct it.

7.15.   After this I proceed to his instruction. I ask him about his illnesses, vices, manner of life, I listen to his heart and lungs, I looked at his body to inspect changes caused by his illness, whatever is visible to the naked eye. I turn especial attention to the reason for his complaints and meanwhile I am attempting to understand what the root of evil is that is causing his body to weaken and summoning the illness, or maybe something else may be wrong with him causing him this illness and he does not know it. From every facet I instruct each person individually until I understand him and discover an approach for each complaint of his and my special approach and the means I select for further tempering. In general the tempering will proceed in the following order:

7.16. I turn to the person with a request for him to stop smoking. If he drinks I request that he stop drinking liquor and also stop sexual excess.

7.17. The objective is for him during the period to restrain himself from all activities and attractions that can weary him, consume him and lead him astray, and that he should balance himself and concentrate all of his attention and strength on the matter of his tempering and healing.

7.18. After this I turn to him with the following request: Find someone, anyone, from the sick or destitute that are around you, who is in desperate need of something, and give it to him, without discredit and pity, something or money or food.

7.19. The one who is too stingy to give something to somebody should not receive anything himself and so will not receive anything from me. If a person has nothing to offer, the judgment does not pertain to him, and he will received what he should.

If a person honestly performs my request, I will assign to him and will request him to perform the following regimen and this will start the actual course of tempering:

7.20. On the day that I assign the person is not to eat or drink anything. The morning and evening before he is to wash his feet and hands with cold water. He must think about me and the tempering to be performed the next day.

7.21. That night he will sleep soundly. I will also meditate on him the entire time and plan my tempering.

7.22.   In the morning after he awakens, I admonish him, become more familiar with his state and ask him to continue this regimen until dinner. I will also observe the same regimen and continue to meditate on his tempering.

7.23.   Each person can undergo the entirety of this regimen regularly without difficultly, and this means that he has the strength to attain his recovery. The person who cannot maintain this regimen or decides to have second thoughts will receive nothing and I will refuse to deal any further with him in the future.

7.24.   The person who maintains the entire regimen to dinner of the second day must go outside into the clean air and must three times inhale and exhale fresh air with his mouth pointing upwards and breathe through his mouth. Mentally he must ask Nature to provide him the same life and health that I have, but there is nothing for me to ask.

7.25.   After this he must migrate to a normal regimen, return to his regular diet of food and drink and not worry about any consequences in his life.

7.26.   After accomplishing all of this the person will feel as though he is new person and should no longer fear Nature and his illnesses. But in order that his strengths and health would progress further toward a better situation he must continue to daily wash his feet, three times take a deep breath, inhaling and exhaling, and never to forget about me.

7.27.   In order to even more strengthen and develop his tempering this person must also in the future, one day each week, complete this regimen and on schedule.

The Complete Year-Long Course of Tempering

7.28.   Over the course of the one-year tempering each person who wants to do this, even the weak and ill person, can be rescued from not just all of his illnesses, strengthen his health, acquire immunity to new illnesses and in general complete tempering against harmful influences of unpleasant condition, but also to develop and verify the resistance of the body in any and all situations at any time of the year. Other than this a person will be able to grasp and learn how to utilize in a practical manner the various conditions and strengths in Nature for his health: air and water, the Earth's crust, the electrical atmosphere, and especially rain, cold, sun, wind, hail and snow. The one-year course of tempering needs to begin in the spring when the entirety of Nature is stimulated and growth begins in the central portion of USSR, and this is about April 25.

The complete one-year course of tempering consists of three parts:

Preliminary part:

7.29.   Familiarize the person with examples, methods, conditions and the program of tempering;
7.30.   His decision, and any questions, and his agreement to take the complete course of tempering;
7.31.   My instruction of the person as an organism and as an individual, and the material conditions of his life, and especially his illness and faults;
7.32.   I create a specialized program just for that person, a prescription for his recovery and tempering for the subject person, and I provide him his first concrete order.

Tempering under my supervision and under my direct assistance:

7.33.   Due to the fact that people are different and their conditions are different, and as a result of this each person requires a special approach and a special prescription for tempering, the complete course for all the people retains some general attributes, and in essence it is one program consisting of 12 stages, each to be completed one month at a time.

7.34.   I ask the person to find someone who is in desperately need of something, and to charitably give it to him out of his own property, and then tell me what particularly it was that he gave.

After this I will assign the following regimen for that month:

7.35.   To daily, in the morning and before retiring, to wash his feet in cold water.

7.36.   Not to drink wine, not to smoke, not to take any narcotics, not to be involved in sexual excess, restrain from profanity, gambling or playing cards, lies, conceit, amusements or entertainment that will lead a person astray, to do all of this to bring the scattered and disrupted strengths of the nervous system, consciousness and volition into order. All of this he can easily achieve, and also with my special help in those situations where the person is unable to deal with his vices and bring himself and his life into order.

7.37.   On the second Saturday after the start of the regimen it is necessary to implement a special regimen lasting 1-1/2 days consisting of abstinence from food, drink, sleep, and etc, just as with the 30-hour course of tempering. During this period the person must think about me and I will think about him; he will delve into his nervous system and all of his organisms using his inner vision and touch, stimulating latent strengths using the current of his living body. After this I will supplement the regular regimen with the exercise of breathing three times with deep breaths, inhaling and exhaling through the mouth in the morning and evening in fresh air, and the best direction is with the wind toward you.

7.38. Meanwhile I have my own regimen to perform, delving with my sense of touch into his body, diagnosing it, and stimulating and rectifying it. After the day of the first special regimen the person will feel an improvement in his condition and with great success, desire and easiness he will continue to perform the regimen assigned him.

7.39. After this he must walk without any head covering in any weather.

7.40. On the following Saturday I will assign him another day of a special regimen and with accompany him in performing it.

7.41. And during the final week of the month he must on his own select one day for a special regimen and he will perform it alone.

7.42. I will be examining his tempering the entire period without interruption.

Subsequent independent work in this region by each person:

7.43. The second month consists of his restoration as a person unified with the Earth's crust and society.

Just as the person's body as a complete organism and its parts appear as a unified whole, the parts are also a unified whole, meaning none can function independently of any other. Likewise not one human organ can normally exist and be healthy if its time with the balance of the body is interrupted, so a person cannot be healthy and strong if his living tie with Nature is weakened and interrupted. For this reason the restoration of a person's health and strength includes not only the restoration of his health, the strength of his body as an organism, but in the restoration of the living tie and his unity with the surrounding environment and Nature.

Since a person does not live like a plant or animal, but indirectly and within the environment of Nature, and lives in a society of humanity, he must first of all materialize the restorative ties of his body as an organism with society in a manner that his life in society will fortify his health and strength, rather than shred or weaken them.

What is most important of all of this is the following:

1. Every person must find and create for himself the most compatible conditions and residence in life, and to not deal with these conditions with fear, repulsion or nervous irritation.

   Wherever this person might live among us he must feel courageous and joyous, and love our Motherland. Love unites and nourishes the strength of life, while fear, repulsion and hate uproot a person out of life, like a flower from the ground.

2. Every person must find for himself a compatible vocation and love his work, and any work with which a person occupies himself, even if it is due to necessity, a person must love, because if the person has a loving attitude toward his work it provides strength, while if a person has an attitude of fear or repulsion toward his work then it will suppress and remove his strength. Even then a necessary and favorite work can also cause harm if his body is incapable of it or intellectually not fit for it. This is why it is necessary to not only to learn to love your vocation, but to learn to work in a manner that it will not disrupt your strengths and not cause harm to your health.

In each individual case, dependant on a person and his work, I can help him love his vocation and for him to work in a manner that it will not disrupt his health and strength, but rather fortify it.

I want to say this on behalf of myself that I am the person who developed this concept on my own: this method of tempering and method of healing, and if one of the two is missing then the other will not flourish or survive.

I am a human but there is nothing special about me, only what Nature has gifted me. It taught me how it is possible to live and utilize concrete means for us to be masters and stand firmly in our spots and wherever possible.

Beginning February 12, 1951, I have been held against my will in a regimen, I work physically, developing my body and not counting it difficult: I break down steel walls for the sake of my body. It is apparent from all of this that I was right when I was confined at Taganka and Lubyanka,[18] where I decided to only walk outside in trousers. I would walk about the place, although only in permitted places, because as far as I am concerned Nature serves a purpose with its strengths.

Here in Leningrad I prepared myself to encounter the winter weather, but each day it seems to back away one day, but it will soon arrive. I am not manufactured from steel or bronze, I am a living human being and I distinctly hear every changing item that my body can hear, like this needle. It enters under my skin and into my body. I feel an electric current, but it affects me little.

I spent an entire month in Department One, they drew my blood, placed me in an x-ray machine but they did not notice any deviation from being completely normal, and even a little on the better side. I should thank the doctors as I am not an ill person, but their attitude is that I am a magician or a prankster if I do not need the help of medical doctors but do all my healing on my own. With my knowledge I deal without them regarding the maladies of the ill. And would you believe that I restored to three of their patients their previous health when I provided my tempering. I warned them to follow my regimen so they would not become ill

---

[18] Prisons in Moscow.

again. These facts speak for themselves: they offered me their gratitude. But doctors were of no benefit in this situation, they only interfere with their administrative bureaucracy and make it more difficult for the ill. I know my strengths and my volition well.

I can do whatever I want in regard to the physical aspects of my work, but I only ask of science, of the Soviet government, to not discard this concept of mine, this method, this work and teaching, because it will be valuable in the future. Any other innovations of theirs will not be able to achieve what I have, and I want to bestow freely to science and to every person all of this, so that the copek a person works so hard to get is not squandered in some hospital and no progress is made on behalf of the ill.

My entire life has been a struggle. I cried at Nature and knocked at its doors until its door opened to me. I learned about the atmosphere and compelled it to submit to me, for it to help me, so I could utilize it to help other people. I guarantee you, so you would know more about me, that I did not just sit in one spot and dream, but I vigilantly investigated and every minute I touched and saw so many destitute who were suffering in their illnesses, and I really wanted to help them. I restored their health. And this is why our modern medicine and science does not want my small gear to rotate their large gear, they want their large gear to turn the wheel. But my gear will still rotate the wheel of medical science and my method will scientifically develop for a person to never suffer from illness.

My concept will prevail. If I did not recognize the truth residing in me I would not have done any of this, but I can see distantly, distantly into the future and hope that it will grasp what I have to offer and start to apply it. A person needs to engender the cognizance of this and utilize it to defeat all of the elements that Nature hurls against it, and when a person achieves this he will not fear cold or hunger, but will receive such an excellent state of health through his central nervous system. The principal point is that he will be master of his body and brain, he will compel the heart to flow blood through the lungs, so the blood will flow faster through the valves and energetically through all the muscles so the white corpuscles would become healthy and strong. All of this is achieved through the air of the atmosphere surrounding us.

What is principle is that with an unclothed body you can see and we can see a chest full of wealth. This condition of our Mother – Nature – is based on air and water, without which no life can be sustained on the Earth's crust. I love this, I love Nature and all of its conditions.

November 2, 1951

1) Почему я стал новатором?

Я стал новатором не потому, что хотел получить много денег и славу. Те люди которые хотят новаторами стать только из за денег и славы могут быть на деле совсем не новаторы а не хорошие люди обманщики людей потому что главное для них ни правда а слава и деньги. Я совсем не из таких людей. В своей работе и исканиях я наоборот отказывался от денег и роскоши в жизни наоборот сознательно шел на терпу, и насмешки, отказывался дать от того, что имеют все люди

Я стал новатором потому что с раннего детства чувствовал в себе силы и стремления совершить что-то особенно, полезное людям хотя и не знал с начало что именно. Я только одно знал с начало что нужно помочь всем бедным страдающим людям и что помощь можно найти и надо искать в чем то новым а не старом и обильным. Я всю жизнь стремился от старого к новому и не бывалому. Я новатор потому что меня

Manuscript of Porfiri Ivanov of the first page of
The History and Method of my Tempering

62

DETKA

I just turned 85 years of age. I dedicated 50 of these years to the practical search of the route of a healthy life. To attain this I daily tested several effects of Nature, and especially its severe facets. I am filled with desires to bestow my experience upon our youth and all Soviet people. This is my gift to them.

Child, you are filled with desires to bring a benefit to our Soviet nation that is building communism. For this reason you need to strive to be healthy.

My heart's request of you is to accept from me some advice to supplement what was already published in order to fortify your health:

1. Twice a day bathe in cold fresh water so you will be refreshed. Bathe wherever you can: in a lake, river, bathhouse, take a shower or pour the water over you. These are your conditions. Replace a hot bath with a cold.
2. Before dining or right after, and if possible do this simultaneously, take a walk into Nature, stand barefooted on the ground, and in the snow during winter, even for 1 or 2 minutes. Breathe fresh air through your mouth several times and mentally wish good health for yourself and others.
3. Do not drink alcohol and do not smoke.
4. Aspire to at least once a week avoid food and water, doing this beginning Friday starting between 6 and 8 PM, until Sunday at 12 noon. This will be to your merit and you will rest better. If it is too difficult then at least try for one day.
5. At noon on Sunday go outside and take a walk barefooted in Nature and heavily breathe several times and contemplate on

what is written above. This is a rest day from your work. After this you can eat all that you want.

6. Love Nature that surrounds you. Do not spit saliva just anywhere and it is best not to spit at all. If you accustom yourself to doing this it will be to your benefit.

7. Greet everyone you encounter and wherever this may occur, and especially with aged persons. If you want to have good health, want good health for other.

8. Help people to the extent you can, especially the poor, ill, underprivileged and oppressed. Do this joyfully. Supplement his needs with your soul and heart, you will make a friend out of him and help the effort of peace.

9. Defeat greed, gratification, lethargy, profiteering, fear, hypocrisy, and pride within yourself. Believe people and love them. Do not speak incorrectly of other people and do not allow the bad opinions of others to infiltrate your heart.

10. Liberate your head from thoughts of illness, depression, death. This is your victory.

11. Do not separate intent from action. If you read about doing something, this is good, but what is principal is to do it.

12. Explain and relate your experience in this matter to others, but do not boast or become haughty. Be contrite.

If something is unclear to you or insufficient in its explanation, then write to me. I am always ready to relate to anyone my experience so that your effort will be successful.

I wish you prosperity and good health.

Porfiri Korneevich Ivanov

The following seven points of Porfiri's concepts and method of tempering were part of an article dealing with Porfiri Ivanov and was printed in Issue 8, 1982, of *Ogonyok*.

1. Live with the constant desire to do good to people, and after you do one thing, do not recollect it anymore, but proceed forward to do another.
2. Aspire to do everything with satisfaction, with enjoyment. Until you learn to act joyfully consider not being able to do it at all.
3. Do not drink wine or vodka.
4. Abstain from food one day a week. During the balance, eat less meat and in general eat less.
5. Walk in the grass and in the snow barefooted all year round and at least for several minutes every day.
6. Bathe in cold water every day, in the morning and in the evening.
7. Spend more time outdoors in the fresh air and with your body open, during summer and winter.

Manuscript of Porfiri Ivanov of the first page of
My Treatment Simplified

TWO ROADS

I maintain only one road and so walk along it. As long as it is, if I absolutely need to wear shoes to traverse it I will greatly tire during this time. As a result I will no longer want to walk along this road. Exhaustion will develop in your body. It will become difficult to live in Nature. Based on this criteria it will be necessary for me to bid farewell to this road. It forces us, you and I, to reject this first road and for us to travel far and further from it.

We have decided to undertake a different road. It is that road where it will be easy for us to live without any footwear. A rug will be laid for you everywhere and in every place. It will not harm our feet, it will not cause any harm to our body. Our body will progress on account of solely Nature, due to natural effects. So these are the two roads.

Along one of them you and I have learned to seek our own eternally littered dependence. But it has provided us a piece of it, although just a rag, and installed a barricade, and led us along its own conviction, its activity and effort, as though all of this will save us. And so we live and continue our life over the years as a result of this. However you and I strongly err if we think this way, or speak this way about our food and our clothes, and likewise for our residence. You and I squander three separate hours each day on this. If we were to eat this food minute by minute all day we would have no time to live. But our bodies are clogged and have not given us the opportunity to live at all. We tend to eat three or four occasions a day, otherwise our body lives on account of rest. Likewise we do not wear the identical clothes and not all the time, so not to wear them out, but wear them depending on [weather] conditions. We remove them when it is hot, and add more if it is cold. If we were to always wear clothes then we would not have the money to purchase new clothing as often as we would need, and what we have would decay on our bodies. Because of its weight they need to be removed. The air of the atmosphere imposes pressure [on clothes] and forces a person's strengths to the ground. This is why a person loses his strengths while walking along the road. He becomes tired while walking all the time wearing clothes and does not go home to rest; even then he just keeps moving all the time at home. He has a stack on his oven to allow ventilation. So the person cooks food for himself and then eats, and then lies in bed and there sleeps soundly with beautiful dreams. On occasion all suffocate due to conditions they create for themselves, and in general a person dies in his home. They carry the coffin from his home and bring it to its assigned place, there, where all of his forefathers lie in the dust of the ground.

Nature is alive and living, not dead, but people speak of what they have never lived.

I WRITE OF NATURE

I write of Nature, its qualities that lead to health. Nature exists so a person does not entirely die. The sage arriving from the east tells you this. He relates to us all the same words, "Woe to you, woe will it be to you people. You lived all over the world in warmth and pleasure. You are scholars, Pharisees and hypocrites." Who gave you to the right to place God in a prison and assign him to a psychiatric hospital? You wanted my body to die for ever and ever. I am not Christ whom you have sentenced and crucified for his virtue. I am God for the Earth who descended to the land for the salvation of humanity's life. I returned to him, to this person, the health he previously had. This is the reason I arose among you in glory. My body is your body. Because of your laws I had to pay a fine, I paid you 30 rubles. You are salesmen dealing in lives, you need money so bad. You have no cognizance, "You are gypsies of a natural character." You fear Nature. However you will answer in the presence of Nature. But it is god that is on the side of Nature, as in the past so at the present there is only one in the world to do this. He is everybody's helper located in sorrow and calamity, and who has no termination and no boundary.

Another started to develop beginning in the year 1898. Now it is 1978, and his turn has arrived. February 20 is the day of the birth of the system – paradise. We sat together at a common table. Here were peasants and workers and along with them a miner, steel maker, and many others: scholars, artists, painters, male and female singers. On a table was a loaf of bread and a few bowls, but we had a good hostess: not only did we eat and drink, but we also learned how to get by without all of this. It was indispensable for everyone who participated to say, "Thank you," and to the old and you. Paradise was restored for us: that which we wanted for our life, that we received, this was the heavenly paradise in spirit. This paradise we created on our own and this is where our happiness resides. This is with what we surrounded ourselves, patience was born in us, this Teacher taught us all. Nature prompted him to say all that was necessary. Now he teaches us and we are his students, new, nonexistent until now, those who do not do what other people do. We end up doing everything from start on our own, and we do not have sufficient fortitude to discard all of this as once we have started we need to complete. It is obvious for the development of our entire technique and science and which is not stationary. This history and Nature compels us to progress toward the Father and Son. But now the Holy Spirit has arrived into our arena, It has envelope his body, sanctified it, and it has become a healthy body, a healthy spirit, because a healthy spirit resides in a healthy body. For people this has long been indispensable. They were awaiting this from the very first beginnings of their life. They asked of It, although the Spirit was unknown to them, and It still helped them.

The Spirit hovered over the waters, but right now it surrounds the person, sanctifies him. He – this person – now helps the underprivileged and sick in voluntary service, he intercedes for them. He wants to tell all of you, "I arrived in your presence to deliver to you all kindness available. I will restore your health so you will have pain no more and become ill no more." Earlier such a work was never started among people. We did nothing to restore their health, and so they continued to die for ever and ever. Our endeavor is not to continue the past and just die, and we will die if we do not change the environment we have created over the course of the entirety of humanity's history.

I was not born for the purpose of creating some important work out of this work, it is the progress of humanity's life that compels all of us to do this. As a result we tightly hold to this work, considering it our own, aspiring to prove that we have the ability to live in a manner that indicates this is indispensable to all of us people. However our health declines to a state of oblivion. But we are unable to act in a manner to discard everything that wants to lead us to death. Earlier death did not exist in Nature. It is a result of the manner we progress in our life that we cause death to develop in us. Nature hated us and so we started to fight against it, and only selected what we found in it that was sweeter and fatter. Nature will only tolerate this to a certain point.

The teacher wanted to honorably accomplish the assignment bestowed on him, but Nature did not want the Teacher to just proceed along some regular route among people. And although he worked with full authority in preparation to do this, administrative people made arrangements for his to be terminated from his employment and categorized him as a class one invalid.

Up to this time I worked during the day, while at night I received the sick. The principal doctor, Davidov, at he railroad hospital in Minvoga[19] gave me access to diagnose the sick there. There I was able to get a woman to stand on her feet, she was lying in isolation as her feet were atrophied. The other sick patients asked for me to remain as they needed a doctor like me, but then the resident doctors asked me to leave the hospital. When they recognize me in the manner that their patients recognize me, then there will be no need for hospitals.

I possessed these strengths earlier. I encountered a woman on Pervomayskoi[20] Street in Elizavetovka,[21] Lugansk Province, and got her on her feet. I walked barefooted along the wet snow with her. Later this woman, who was lying down and needed to walk, herself prepared something for me and her children to eat. My brother-in-law Feodor Feodorovich was a witness to this and can verify it. I went to the Executive Committee of the City Soviet, to the Department of Education, to a man named Ivanov (same name

---

[19] Mineralnye Vody, or Mineral Springs, a town in Stavropol District, along the Kuma River, and 400 miles southeast of Krasni Sulin, Porfiri's home.

[20] First of May

[21] A small city just west about 10 miles of Dnipropetrovsk.

71

as myself, but not related). He summoned several doctors based on my request and explanation, but all they did was decide to assign me to the local psychiatric hospital. I barely got away from them. While walking on the road to Krasni Sulin, I saw high in the sky an airplane used for agricultural purposes. Then I thought to myself, that if this airplane lands near me, then my concepts are correct. So what did I see next? The airplane all of a sudden started to drop and then descended and landed near me. I walked up to the pilot and asked, "What is the matter?" The pilot tells me, "A mechanical problem." I walk further and see two roads: one to the right and the other to the left. Which of them should I take to get home? I stand and wait... And suddenly on the right side a man as though appears from nowhere. He walks up to me... I excuse myself to him and ask him the best route to take to end up in Sinelnikovo.[22] He points to the same road along which he was traveling. I went along the road he indicated while thinking to myself, "I need to look at him once more." I turned around and there was no trace of him, and all that surrounded us was an open and flat field, with not one hollow or mount. Nothing like this had ever occurred to me. I just asked myself what he was and if I would ever understand.

Getting closer to home I stopped to visit a friend named Shvartz. The day before I was able to get a woman named Evdokia Pankratevna on her feet. She did not walk for five years as her feet were atrophied. I did not just abandon my tempering, but sometimes I would take the sick to a local medical office. When I did that here, they decided that I meet with some of the doctors. I spoke with them in length at the medical clinic, and Dr Shishov was there with them. I was hoping for some support from them, but instead they called the police and escorted me out of there. I was walking along the houses in Syatovo,[23] when my sister-in-law

---

[22] A small city in Dnipropetrovsk Province, Ukraine, about 30 miles east of the city Dnipropetrovsk. His home at Krasni Sulin is another 300 miles to the east.

[23] A city in Svatovski District, Lugansk Province, about 200 miles north of his home in Krasni Sulin.

tells me, that the doctors told the police that when I was at the clinic I broke the windows.

I did not abandon my practice. People called me pope, as I had long hair.[24] The rumor spread that as if I quit working on my own, but it was the decision of the committee for me not to work six months. During the entirety of the six months I helped people and returned their health to them. I did all of this for the sake of the people. However I still have to work. I went to the governor of the province and he helped me get a job. I did my best to earn an honest living, however people surrounding me interfered with me. They cut my hair from behind my back and then terminated me. What am I supposed to do? They would throw me in the sea to drown me if they could.

My concepts need to live and develop, but they have turned it into something abnormal and wanted to mortify it. This is what the "wise of the world" in this province did, this doctor and psychiatrist Artemyev, and he is still alive. But I was not afraid of this, and went home and shattered all of these superficial barricades into smithereens. I had in my possession a document regarding the state of my health issued by the Serbski Institute and signed by the supervision Vvedenski. This was my atomic bomb, my defense. As long as I had this document I was not afraid of wandering through Nature and preserving my health. And all the people I encountered loved me for it. They would provide me shelter, provide me charity on which to survive. Some local workers' unions were also willing to provide me financial assistance. All of these people, whoever they were, regardless of nationality and religion, they were willing to do anything within their means for me, they were my strength. I extended myself for their behalf, and this did the same for me, because we all need to be healthy.

People send search parties after me and say, "We need to do this. We are always looking for him, we never stop." Two

---

[24] The priests of the Russian Orthodox Church did not cut their hair or beards.

variations of this statement have circulated. The Father and Son we buried, and now in exchange for them the Holy Spirit is arriving. He is a person who will envelope you from the inside and outside and give life to a person, while the person with constant effort and endurance while on the route of union with the Spirit will save himself. We should have said this about this person a long time ago, as he is an unstable solitarian, but now at the present he is finally disclosing himself to the public.

The year of 1978 has arrived! All of us living in the world and those who lived before us have accomplished much effort, but to acquire from all of this some satisfaction, this we have not received.

All those residing throughout this wide world, they all stand in line waiting for their day. When that day comes they will become seriously ill and die for always just as all those before them died.

They all lie in their dust and wait for when the man who will arrive from the east will raise them. He will relate his words to all of us, "Woe to you, woe to you scholars, Pharisees and hypocrites. The churches are desolate, the gift of God is lost, your positions are gone." He will tell all of us, "So how have you lived?" But we in unison will answer him in this manner, "We lived comfortably and in warmth." And he will respond, "And whom did you abandon to live destitute and in the cold. You did this to me, and doing nothing of what I requested of you, you retained all that was yours close to you, and you called your residences your own. But where is the place for me? You gave me no place to reside. So now go and live in your own that you have build for yourselves, but do not interfere with me. I have no need for what is yours. What you have to offer me does not align with my soul or my heart. Yours is yours and mine is mine! Your cognizance had defined your existence so that you only live for your selves, just as you did earlier. The time will come when you will complain to me, but then I will be silent to your pleas."

All people are ill, that is, they maintain deficiencies, they want much but room is not provided them, but once people think that they have nothing to gain, this is their insufficiency, and if they receive nothing, then this evolves into illness, and sometimes the worst, and then they die in this insufficiency.

But what was first born of it had no need of anything. Surrounding him laid much that was living, energetic and much that was yet to be started. He was the God of all of this and preserved this wealth. The Spirit dedicated him, just as with our dear Teacher. So he is right now!

And not one person of all those living in the world did what he did to deliver people from all that is not life in the world. The Teacher took this responsibility on himself. As a result of this Nature gifted him, it provided him strength, taught him how to utilize this. To be polite in the presence of all, this is the first task, to place yourself in the service of others!

On February 11, 1978, on television, there was a documentary on God, whom no one and at no time has seen. But why do they portray Him in this manner for our young people? Weren't these nuns dedicated to His cause? He always had in His presence Angels to accomplish His will, they were the materializers of all activities in the atmosphere, that is, in the ether.[25] However all was not in the manner they displayed this on television if we were to align it with history which records events before the beginning of God as we know Him. There was no darkness and there was no light. Tell all the scholars, artists and everybody directly, "What existed earlier, before when there was no light or darkness, but God already existed in your history?"

You don't know, you cannot do anything, you have no responsibility, and great sorrow will befall you scholars, Pharisees and hypocrites. A person will arrive from the east to confront you on all you have concocted. He will explain the matter, be he will not be believed. But the time will come, they will desolate the churches, the gift of God will depart, He will no longer be among us. But we are people of pride, we will boast of our life, and in this

---

[25] This was the manner that the atheist Soviet populace would refer to heaven.

manner, that we have created it and reside well and warm, and it is not technology or art or chemistry that created all of this, but our personal effort.

So to where did the Holy Spirit depart, if Nature as a natural occurrence resides in It?

People wanted to depart from all of this and did throughout history only what they felt needed to be done. And their work led them to what they earned and deserved – DEATH!

But right now a person will arrive on the scene. Nature will summon him, it will teach him how to help a person who resides in sorrow and destitution. He will earn Nature's trust that he is sincere and reliable, and so people will believe him as being such. He will depart from them and to the sea, while they will remain on dry land. He will walk on water. This is necessary to do among people.

Nature speaks, "I am the birth mother, this applies to all of you in the same manner. What I want I will accomplish among people. So am I in all areas your birth mother upon whom you depend, and know that I alone have provided all of you birth. But what did you do? Install a new order for your selves, to begin your life from the summit of the mountains, and then later slide down the mountain and to your destruction. And we know nothing else other than this. This is to what people gave birth. We do not know where to begin, we have no comprehension to attribute to our account.

The human evolved from God, and as considered among people, he was initially assembled and then they blew Spirit into him and he completed his formation as a human. But God, being who He is, has not been seen by any person and He is not visible in order to be seen. He is this something else in life of which a person can only surmise. He has servants that were born in Nature. They started to believe in God, but others started to think that it was not this way in life at all and so started to think in this other manner. So there are two directions in our wide world, but this is not good.

Once they did not provide to the human the possibilities for him to accomplish his assignment then this was no longer life. So is the history of humanity: a father had two sons. One obeyed the father, the other did not. One wanted to always stay close to home, the other wanted to always leave home. However father is still father and he attempted to gratify the both of them, not to insult the one and not to abandon the other. He did not object to what his sons were doing. The obedient and diligent son that honored the father, the father kept close to him, while the disobedient who demanded his portion of the inheritance, was likewise not denied his request and was given his portion. Once receiving his portion he departed for wherever he wanted and so he squandered all of his wealth and became destitute. He then went to find work at the estate of some rich person and work under his supervision, although it was very difficult for him to do this. He remember his natal father and decided to return and get hired as a servant. As father is father he felt sorrowful for his disobedient son. He was overjoyed at his repentance and for the sake of his safe return he held a feast and did not spare anything for the event as he was very rich. But his second son was in the field during this time and working hard. He learned of his brother's return and of the feast held in his honor and provided by his father. This annoyed him and so he reprimanded the father for showing this kindness. But the father said to his son, "Pardon him, son, forgive him for acting insolently. You and I will somehow settle the matter later. No one will have the opportunity to accuse you of acting this way, or me. We have done right to accept your brother on his return. It is good he remembered me, and he also remembered you." So was the history of the event.

Can we actually stop this history at this point? It began with people and it ended with people. But for some reason people have no comprehension at all of this event. They are all psychologically ill: they only want to be given something, and understand no more. They retain in their mind and heart one thing – a personal benefit. And when they acquire a profit, they cannot live anymore, they die.

I arrived as your Teacher and want to tell you about this.

Know that all that we have done in our life, and especially at the present, is death for us. Death as a result of this matter! But more than one person in his life has escape this death and walked away from it, and as if this is not what people expected or wanted. But they have not done anything for their life as they are all consumed in this general trend of things that lead to death. However people have selected the one route of living well and warm, and started to depart from the poor and cold. This is what people have done in Nature: not to display their love, but instead display their whims, wants and dissatisfaction.

However this did not provide a person any satisfaction because he did not like Nature to the extent he should and did not value it enough, but on the contrary, finding it to be alive he pursued it with his weapons and killed it. Who will have pity on you for committing such a crime? Know that blood is paid for with blood. You did it to Nature today, and it will impose the same on you tomorrow.

People's hopes seem to always rely on – perhaps. A person lives well he is happy, a person lives poorly he weeps. But for this not to occur we have not earned our merit from Nature for matters to not be so simple. For all the wrong that we have done, it has fallen upon us with its bacteria or fungi, not having the means to escape from it and so we die. This is what we have merited from Nature, and no one specific person is to blame for this but only people with their history.

We accomplished the revolution on our own in order to deliver ourselves from private property which is to blame for everything. But prior to this time, that is, during the monarchy, the father left his property to the son. Now Soviet authority has entered into the role of the son, inviting scholars for them to teach grammar to this son, establish him theoretically, so he would be a technical person among people, for everything to become artificial with the help of chemistry, for it to be well and warm for people. Many gave their lives for such conditions.

However up to this point it is not obvious that the scholars have accomplished something useful for true life. They have developed what is technological and artificial using their knowledge and effort with the help of chemistry. But this does not help life, but actually interferes with it. What is necessary if for the scholar to undertake this endeavor without any monetary interests, and then he can migrate to a practice of being a benefit to people. Enough of this introduction of technology, enough of making everything artificial, enough of this progress in chemistry. We need to achieve this one something from Nature: to live in it on account of environment, on account of practical application. Know that we should not die, but rather live. We need to gain the capacity to dominate these natural strengths that serve life. They do exist in Nature and it is indispensable for us to utilize them. And these are not some kinds of alien artificial strengths, these strengths must be natural and they do exist in Nature! There is nothing stronger than the elements of Nature, it is principal. Whatever it wants, this it does and it has the natural strengths to do it. I have spoken of them to many scholars. I ask them, "Tell me, please, what existed before light and darkness existed? What was there for an atmosphere?" But these scholars do not know and cannot state anything in this regard. But know that they have accepted this assignment and it has provided no benefit of any kind for people. We have lost our health, and so in this state we have dug graves for ourselves in the ground and we now lie in the dust. And no one other than the Teacher thinks about help this dead individual.

And he needs help because in Nature that surrounds us nothing is futilely discarded, all has lived and is living eternally in Nature. This is more than just a hill of beans.[26] In order to achieve all of these endeavors Nature has sent this person to us, a certain

---

[26] English equivalent of the Russian cliché: This is more than a pound of raisins.

individual who is full of life and joy maintaining a thought and activity pertaining to the whole universe residing in Nature. His body arrived recently and inaugurated a new beginning. We likewise in our own effort delay a termination, so he would also arrive here to initiate a new beginning. However Nature will not provide him to us as it wants to return everything backwards. The time will come: who buried the person will unearth him! People will be healed just at the mention of one word. They are awaiting this themselves when they will enter through one set of doors and leave healthy through the next sets of doors. And no sooner will this be achieved that they will resurrect people from this state they are in. Then the opportunity will finally arrive for me to occupy my spot in glory, and then likewise reprimand people for their violations. For doing this I will receive every manner of trust, and so can judge people for their mistakes.

I am Parshek[27] pertaining to this entire matter. Nature is entrusted to me. It has sanctified me as a result. In this matter I am god. Since it is this way you much believe him. He came to you from the east and to relate all of this to you! Yes! Yes! There will be a termination to this, as for all that we have done, he will condemn us. Where has all the good that we have done, all that was given us from Nature, gone? We have not wanted for another what we have wanted ourselves. We have not clothed the naked, or fed the hungry, or assisted the needy, or comforted the suffering. We have not seen this person, but for us to want him, we have nothing to show that we did. And he will ask us, "How did you live?" We will answer him in this manner, "We worked, accumulated money, ate, drank, dressed warmly, and lived comfortably in our home." And they he will tell us, "Well then, go ahead and live how you want. So even if I am cold and destitute, don't waste your time on me. I am not interested in your matters

---

[27] This is a nickname applied to Porfiri Korneevich when he was an adolescent, but he takes advantage of it here.

and do not want to become what you are. I do not want to live in the manner that you live. I do not want to be a scholar, Pharisee and hypocrite and wanting others to do this while I do something else. You buy Nature and you sell Nature. What you are doing is a big joke. You want to prove that you are people excessively educated. But Nature is Nature and it teaches a person not to worry about tomorrow. A person has not yet even lived and he is already preparing himself for greater matters. He already has this preconceived thought in his mind regarding what he intends to do tomorrow and day after tomorrow and so forth, and no end to his preconceived preparations. But to do something correct in life, in order not to err, a person is not capable of doing this. Regardless of all of his technology, design, chemistry, he could not do anything without making a mistake."

The following event occurred in my history. During icy rain I walked passed a column of machines that were sliding people upwards.[28] I walking along it barefooted and was able to catch up to those riding on these machines, and then continued further on my travel. I am not a technological person, but I said what I had to say. If right now you were to banish from Nature all the technology implemented by humanity, then it would be powerless. Being powerless provides no movement forward, while Nature, regardless of any technology, helps everybody on the road. Nature preserves only the naturally living person!

At the beginning of winter I was traveling by Tuapse. A storm ensued of unbelievable force, no less than 12 on the Beaufort scale. Even telegraph poles were being toppled. But I was not afraid of entering these immense turbulent waves. But just as I walked into the water, the sea immediately calmed. This was the beginning of my life-long route. I ate nothing at the time and did not even take food with me. Over the course of 12 days I walked in the sea and sat on the shore. On occasion I would walk into the

---

[28] Probably a ski lift or something similar.

sea at night. I would sit in the water and listen how trains would be rolling by past me. I submerged myself into the water, I saw the most different kind of light ever of blinding intensity, and more than in any home I was in. [29]

This is really what I experienced, it started November 23, and on December 5, I arrived in Sochi. If you only saw the amount of snow the Nature loaded on me when I arrived in this city. I walked through it like Holy Spirit. I was surrounded by snow from my feet to the top of my head, like white feathers. People followed me to the very shore of the sea. Then they compelled me to enter the water and so deep that I was completely submerged, but I do not remember how long I was under water. I only recollect that those who rescued me pulled me out in their nets and I was alive and unharmed. They took me to the police station. It is a good thing that I still had my documents in my pant's pocket regarding the condition of my mental health, that I was well. They took me to the train station and put me on the next train out, so I would not lead any more people astray with what they labeled as a prank. I met with some government representatives. I told them of my practices, I explained to them about the truth of my endeavors. I want all people to verify this experience as being a live incidence occurring in the presence of other people.

During Hitler's invasion of Russia with his superior forces, my place of residence was under occupation by Hitler's troops. I met [Friedrich] Paulus. He asked me, "Who will win?" I answered, "Stalin." He became familiar with my concepts and gave me a directive, first composed in Russian and then also in German and attached his personal imprint on it to validate it. It was due to this order that I was able to survive the German occupation of

---

[29] What he means is that he was on the shore of the Black Sea the entire time and exposed directly to the elements of the hurricane while in the water. This is probably the same event where he was on the deck of a ship exposed to the elements, and got the details confused. But in the next paragraph he states he arrives in Sochi, or maybe he was walking from Tuapse to Sochi. Porfiri is hard to follow.

Ukraine and southern Russia. The Germans that noticed I was in good terms with Paulus, shouted, "Hurray," while the German officers decided to transfer me to Berlin. They placed me in a railroad car together with recruits and we left the area. But for some reason I was removed from the train and taken into custody by Ukrainian police, although they did not know my concepts. Those police from Znamenski took me to Dnipropetrovsk, to the Gestapo. During the entire incident I was unharmed and arrived there safe, since it was Nature that protected me.

I talked with some of their soldiers while traveling but through an interpreter. They also shouted, "Hurray." However even with the complements the German soldier took me using his weapon and then brought me to the commander. They had a motorcycle and they toured me, attired solely in trousers, all over the city all night in the piercing frost and wind. But I was not harmed, not one bit. I asked Nature to get me a Russian soldier who will rescue me from this German, and so this occurred! Nature heard my request and helped this one Russian soldier to win over the German and rescue me.

The German army lost its superiority near Moscow and started its withdraw. I sat at the Gestapo for 27 days and during the entire time did all that I possible could to gain our victory. I conveyed my thoughts from my mind and had them crawl into Hitler's head, and so behind his back I stimulated him to make decisions that would end in defeat for fascist Germany. These fascist officers, political scoundrels, asked me, "Who will win?" I responded, "Stalin." The Germans lost the war and so provided merit for Parshek who asked Nature to do what was necessary for the Russian soldier to win. However Parshek is not in favor of people killing each other. He is in favor of terminating war on both sides, he is on the side of peace! He advocates love between all nations, and which only can bring us to eternal life without death.!

Now let me tell you about the enemy that is internally and externally located in people and which is engendered by people. We cannot fathom it and will never be able to fathom it, although it exists. We have overthrown kings, defeated the monarchy, that is, exchanged the father for the son, introduced science, art, chemistry, in order to become independent from Nature. But just as the enemy was among us in the past, the external and so the internal, so it remains among people. Because people barricaded themselves from Nature, they now are powerless in Nature. They established their reliance on the lifeless: technology, art, chemistry. All that they do has the intent of appropriating what they can from Nature, and only what they need for themselves, for their personal interests that were defined by people at the beginning of their life and which has always led and will always lead to one termination: death.

But just now a person arrived from the east. He has a pragmatic and natural character, he has won over Nature and a Teacher of the nations, the God for the Earth. He was naturally able to gain control over Nature, he was able to acquire people's trust in him. Nature will help him in every area and provides him the life-creating strengths that reside in him.

All of this has been prepared over the past two millennia. But meanwhile our Earth pertains to all of us people residing in the whole wide world, and all that we have done upon it we have utilized for our own purpose and yet not satisfied ourselves. We are just people, all of us lie in our places in the dust. These people lie there and await my name, awaiting for me to raise them all from there, and not only to raise them, but to compel them, to the very last one, to answer for all they have done. This will be absolutely indispensable and something they have earned on their own. They will surround Nature and it will gift them life-providing strengths and enlighten them forever and ever.

I wish you all happiness, health and all the best.

February 14, 1978

THE TEACHER

MY GIFT TO YOUNG PEOPLE

I look into the distance, I see much that is ahead of me. But this is how it was during my younger years, I was 20 years of age at the time and right now I am 85 years of age and I am still looking into the distance. In our village there was a gang at each end and they would fight each other in the streets. They would chase after us in our area and beat us up. Once Emilian Fedotovich Kobzev is walking by, he is hurt and in pain, he talks to me as though complaining: they are beating us up and asks me to somehow help, but on their side is their fighter Marko Mamonov, none of the men from our side of he village was able to defeat him. So the occasion arose for me to encounter him one on one. I punched him right in the center of the chest, he collapsed and flew backward and then the boys from our end chased him away. After the fight I returned home.

But right now in front of me international problems are disclosed – somehow to implement peace on Earth, and in the entire world. How is the activist Porfiri Korneevich Ivanov, a teacher of the people and who considers himself having won over Nature, supposed to implement his tempering and procedure derived from Nature to do this? The young people of the world are divided into our socialist and their capitalist, and they need to admit blame and condescend, ask forgiveness for the mistakes they have made, not to distrust one another or maintain hostility. I will help you, I will show you my love in the presence of Nature, I will speak on behalf of cold weather, that it is a lifetime friend and will help you at any time. Even in the worst of times or the worst of places I will not abandon you when you are in need. This process is not mine, it is derived from paradise, and its merit on behalf of humanity is immortal. For 50 years I have traveled and contemplated, acted, and have not found an easier or better system than this one. My task is to assist each and every person to the extent I can.

It is the obligation for all of us to love mother Nature, to value it, preserve it as the apple of our eye, then pain and illness will no longer play a role in humanity. We need to learn Ivanov's concepts so we do not end up in jail or on a bed in some hospital, but to live in freedom from pain and illness. My dear native people, look at the sun, you will see virtue, your restoration and so become Nature's winners, Teachers of the Nation, and Gods of earth.

We, the people of all the world, want and we will accomplish, and we will succeed. Nature has assigned a place for us. This place is the Chuvinski Hill.[30] All of the requirements of our life for all young people are available there. We need to grasp this opportunity for all of our people, all young people. We will proceed to this hill as one group and barefooted and Parshek will be with us. In unison we will proclaim this place as our paradise. Yes, we will attain with you. If we will do what solely Nature assigns us, will not descend into death. Our leader is Parshek,[31] he is our landmark. Parshek bows low to everybody, asks all of us to accept this assignment and work in Nature without end and to the end, and then we will not die. Life as we knew it will return.

The tempering teaches us, that we and all of you young people should encounter it as our Parshek. It speaks to all people of a trustworthy character. They know well about God, that He resides

---

[30] A place not far from Porfiri's birth city Orekhova.
[31] Referring to himself

in our life, and we need to firmly believed that He is what He is. But ask them how they observe His dictates. He said with His own words, "Do not want for someone what you do not want for yourself."[32] If it is not your intent to observe this, then it is better to not believe in God at all. So with Parshek the thoughts materialized, "God is God, and so do not act bad as a result of this." A person needs to display himself in public in his activities to indicate that you are god in Nature. People will recognize you as a god, and so will ask you to help them in all things. This is god, and you, Parshek, ask the youth, let them approach you as a god to ask for advice, then there will not be any war, but peace in all the world, peace in all the world. He arrived on Earth to banish this type of death, while introducing a life that maintains a glory. When people decide to ascend this hill, they will loudly announce their convictions. This place is our paradise, and immortal merit on behalf of humanity.

Parshek raises all the dead, and he will not allow the living to descend into the ground. The younger generation can continue this process. They will walk barefooted on the ground and proclaim this as the manner to proceed. Once this occurs the land will no longer be ploughed, but it will grow flowers on its own and its fragrance will fill the air. No longer will a bad odor exist.

Evolution will provide the youth a route, the Holy Spirit will surround them, wisdom will enter the arena, credit applied to all of them will cause the gates to open. The new person will remain there to live forever and ever.

Nature has traversed the planet, sought and saw very many, but not one person of all of those residing here agreed to undertake this endeavor and follow after it. All were occupied with their own affairs. So how did I manger to do this, traverse it for 50 years? I was not afraid of Nature, as a result of applying my own method of tempering on myself I walked winter and summer barefooted

---

[32] Tobit 4:15

with nothing but shorts. I have accomplished this and will continue, I will not discard my goal. I retain the Holy Spirit and will retain it along with the entire history of the evolution of all life, so that all will become new in all the world.

I alone in the wide world labor for the welfare of all people. I learn in Nature, I boast of this to the world, I truly want to speak on behalf of the preservation of my body. My heart, it is young and sturdy, a healthy heart the same as a person 25 years of age. This is how I entered society. I am not afraid of any enemy and anyplace, even my death. If it was not this way I would have died long ago. I was derived from the soil, I breathe soundly, and speak sharply but not in regard to some miracle, but on behalf of Nature, for its physical and practical manifestation. This is principal: inhaling and exhaling clean air, stimulation in the snow, the immediate healing of the central nervous system and the brain. I love helping the ill, I know his heart and his soul, I want to help him, with my hands I touch him and I defeat the pain. These are just not words we speak to all the people, but all is accomplished by effort. My hand writes and so correctly, but what is my petition? My request is for you to be well. To whom does this apply? To our young people? Yes and No, as this has worldwide significance. We need to love mother Nature, value it, preserve it like the apple of our eye. While illness afflicting a person should have no roll at all, the only roll is that of a person over illness. Sometimes my life is difficult. Comprehend my conscious patience, train your hearts. Look upon the sun, you will see virtue, your healing to be just as I am: Conqueror over Nature, Teacher of the Nation, God for the Earth.

Discard your previous form of life, the obsolete person decaying in circumstances of lust and rather be renewed by the spirit of your mind and be clothed into a new person created after the image of the God of virtue and holiness of truth. The Bible raises an interesting question. What manner must we live in order to provide a useful life? Ignoring the deficiencies of the world, people still in general maintain an aspiration toward goodness, toward a knowledge of God. No one has yet succeeded in installing a barricade stopping the influx of benevolent and divine thoughts into the world. So where is the pledge of goodness contained and how can we live a virtuous life? The Bible answers in this manner, "Discard your previous form of life, the obsolete person, and be clothed as a new person."[33] We need to reject one form of life and accept the other, in other words, God becomes our decision and activity. Our decision is to discard the obsolete person. All of us are aware of the obsolete person residing in us, so the Apostle Paul does not consider it necessary for us to be friendly with it, as it is our companion since childhood anyway. It seems to want to receive every temptation available and is ready to so any bad possible, materializing as the enemy of our conscience and diving summons.

Sin is a massive deception and our corporeal person is ready to believe in this deception, yet we do not want to rely on God. How easy it is for the obsolete person to deceive us. The young person thinks that he has fallen into the hands of the tempter due to lack of experience. Young and inexperienced they talk looking for excuses. This is also a deception. Every fall occurs due to a lack of belief. God's Word would have warned this young person and placed him on the proper route, but he did not believe it. What warned him was his individual conscience, but he did not turn his attention to it either. The opinion of intelligent and experience people also warned him, but he felt that they did not understand him. So he fell not due to ignorance, not because he did not see the proper route, but because he did not maintain trust toward what was right. As little as experience helps in sins it unveils a plain fact that those who fall do not just fall once, but a second and then a third time. The corporeal flesh draws a person to the edge of the cliff and ruthlessly throws him down and right to the bottom. Experience in sin does not deliver, but experience in God delivers.

---

[33] Col 3:9-10

Recognize that this is the deception of sin and which compels you to at least once experience sin in the interests of experience and wisdom. This deceptive illusion plays its game while you are at the edge of ruin, just as it was at the time of the Apostle Paul, those various sorceries that deceived people at the time, and which continues to deceive and lead people astray today.[34] Even at the present this brilliant display of gold and jewels, superficial beauty, manipulations and the numbing effect of liquor, artificial smiling, facing and fancy clothes, have not brought happiness just as in the past. Deceptive enticements leading toward foolish conduct continue from the past and to the present, and will until the moral basis that is underneath and below his feet will finally rise to the top and stand firmly upright. This will allow the person to be cleansed of sin. After the first fall a voice will whisper to him softly in his heart, "It is too late." But this is the deceit of sin.

Now the Bible enters into the life of the person gone astray, and it witnesses that the person can proceed along a route of virtue. But if his sins he still has a means of escape from his situation. At any level of collapse deliverance still exists, but only under the conditions that the person immediately makes a decision: Discard the obsolete person.

God awaits this decision from us, and if the person turning to God should return to the path of ruin, he must again make this decision. Without decision there is no salvation.

God counts on us to have the intention of making this decision. "I will arise and go to my Father," said the prodigal son. Only after such a decision could a new life begin in him. During his life in this world Jesus said, "Who wants to fulfill His will will comprehend." In another place the Lord said, "Let the one who desires come and take the water of life free."

The experience of thousands of believing persons proves that one decisive moment can change an entire life and belief for many long years. One moment in Damascus was all it took to change

---

[34] Acts 16:16

Saul, the persecutor of Christians. So what can a present performance of ecclesiastical services do for your life? What can occur to you as a result of a present encounter with Christ? I know that it is difficult to believe in a moment's healing, that this is all the time needed for us to become new people. But believe firmly and steadily. Be ready this very minute and then the Lord will be ready to provide to you. Tell God that you believe in His power to liberate you from servitude to sin. At that moment the culmination of the antagonism of the flesh against the spirit will begin. The obsolete person will protest, but you need to estrange it, to discard it. Accept your decision and entrust yourself to God will your entire self, then the effectiveness of God and His strength will be displayed in your life, and you will no see more your previous sinful life, nothing more captivating or attractive, and out of joy you will be ready to reject it. The work of God is renewal.

Our responsibility is to discard the obsolete person and then God through His power will accomplish in us a new person. But if a person should attempt to liberate himself from sin using his personal strength, through his individual efforts, he will sooner or later be forced to admit, "The desire to do good is in me, but I am unable to do this." However the Lord provides us strength to be clothed in a new person created after the likeness of God.

To be clothed in a new person is the same as to be clothed in Jesus Christ. The new person now exists and there is no reason for us to further seek him. Our sole task is to accept him, the one now created after the likeness of God. The initial person was created after God's image, but he did not remain this way long. The second person who was presented in the world as God's image was Jesus Christ. At the end of his life Jesus Christ presented himself to us as a hero who fought against sin, not in favor of life so much as against death, and he won. The third person after God's image is the new person in us born from above by the Holy Spirit. Not one person in God's eyes can live a life of total value if this new person is not residing in him, and the one who is created after God's likeness, in virtue and in the holiness of truth, should not fear living a life of total value. The new life derived from God now resides in us, but this is not all.

The removal of the obsolete person and attire in a new and original person is a simultaneous event. The word *attire* signified a positive effort. The removal of the obsolete person is a decisive incident occurring during our conversion and attire as a new act of God during rebirth. This new life is continually being renewed, just as our physical life, and is preserved until such time that the renewal occurs in it. The Apostle Paul writes that the inner person is renewed day after day, attired in a new person that is renewed according to the image created by our secret strength, our spiritual life in God.

So we need to discard the obsolete person, assign it to death, as the Bible commands, and through faith devote ourselves and place ourselves in the Lord's hands. Then he will renew us day after day. Our spiritual life is now tied with the source of strength – the Holy Spirit.

We have presented our entire self to God and the door of our heart is widely opened for Him. Do you believe, renewed person, that you are now liberated from servitude to the obsolete person? Know that you are now created for virtue and the holiness of truth. Or do you consider this to be unattainable to you? But know that it says right here that you cannot do this yourself, but God can. So believe that God, who supernaturally provided you a rebirth, will in this supernatural image let you into all that He has promised you in glory. God summons us today to discard the obsolete person, to reject him and accept the new person. This is the sole route that is assigned by God to conquer sin and achieve renewal. God summons us and provides us strength to deal with this difficult task.

That I became god over people was not personally dependant on me. When they stand in front of me in their sorry and distress and ask that I provide them a resolution to their request then I stand in their presence as god. So it will be accomplished, and quite well in real terms, and he will no longer suffer as a result of my effort. As god I must satisfy his petition in a real manner, and he must remain after the occasion completely satisfied. You need to ask me as god in order for you to be satisfied with the event.

Do you want war to terminate among you, ask me as god and war will cease. All of you people, will be able to endure pain and chill, and you will not prematurely die through me as god. Through gods we will become god based on our conduct. God does not command a person to smoke tobacco, drink wine, God does not command us to use profanity or be malicious toward another person. God is courteous toward all people, beseeches them for them to do what is principal in life: want health for all. If you find a person in need help him to the extent you can. The Teacher of all the world is the God for the Earth. He unveiled the light to all and the Holy Spirit shined in people. Then will we all become gods in Nature and in life. All of us will live in Nature easily and with a life full of joy. In order for all to be gods, we need to assist everyone, and so attain to being gods.

This method of tempering asks all of us children for us to know God and for us to become gods in Nature. When all of us absorb this method of tempering, then we will love Nature just as Parshek loves it, and we will then become just the same as he is. We will become gods as a result of the efforts and he will bring all of them into an order, all of us as one entity will love Nature and preserve it. We will be gods of life. This is the method of tempering, it will triumph and will reside with us. There will be no enemy among us as Nature will love us all, and it will provide us all that we need in our life. We will earn this, and an atmosphere of strength will surround us, provide us great glory in our life. Through Nature we will banish death from our life.

This method of tempering will provide us all of this and play and important role in our life, and we will resurrect as living from among the dead and the power of Parshek will surround us. He will be the principal god and leader. To attain this he traversed this route 50 years.

I wish you people happiness, health and goodness.

February 2, 1983

The Teacher Ivanov

MY TREATMENT SIMPLIFIED

I am a human and there is nothing special about me, only what Nature has gifted me. It taught me how it is possible to live and utilize concrete means for us to be masters and stand firmly in our position and wherever possible. We need to learn how we must live in order to possess a prophylactic to protect us from the effects of chill and illness. There is nothing more beautiful than life, and all that is good and pretty in a person is unthinkable without the person's health.

To be healthy is a great benefit. The short interval of the human life should not be a normal situation. It should not be wasted on illnesses. A person must content for his health and continuation of life, but all we have learned is to easily squander our health and with our conduct we just shorten life.

I started to study the reasons for those items that interfere with our health. So why does a person live for a while and then dies? Nature declared the answer to me: People life, utilize rights and eat and are clothed and live in a house and so factually die. People live in life-depriving conditions and this is the response to the question of life-prolongation: we need to live in the natural environment, that is, air, water and earth. Our life depends on air, water and earth. The earth provides us subsoil that produces an abundant harvest for us. We sell this off this way and that way, and then we buy what the law imposes on us.

All people living in this wide world of ours work and defend themselves artificially, they satisfy themselves with items manufactured chemically and replace them as they wear out. They do this in order to lose themselves in it, and these products, no matter how much advertising forces them on us, are harmful to our health, and it seems that life for a human cannot exist without every one of these products available or utilized. So a person proceeds on a route that is harmful, exploit the soil, kill animals. This is a murderous facet of human existence. We initiated this type of life, started to eat until we overeat, clothe ourselves until we are more than just warm, and we reside in homes that have more comforts than we really need. All of this is a great mistake. We are people of old character not wanting what is really valuable for the existence of humanity, and we have gone astray from that route we should be on to reach the goal we should be seeking.

We all have our shortcomings, we have pain and illness with you. When a person is ill, he is suffering some deprivation, not to mention the deprivation that is eventually death. Take a look at your living conditions, it seems all that is mortal surrounds you, your state is one of lifelessness. Walls around you suppress life, windows do not allow air. We need to reject all of this, all of what we are doing, and instead do what will benefit us all. Train ourselves, temper ourselves, work on ourselves, control ourselves, and not to forget others. With this kind of conduct we will become a new type of person, and no longer an ill one. The new person with tempered strengths will not have need of anything, anywhere or of any type. They you will be able to say to others that you have become an independent individual.

By starting on this path of departure a person can have his previous health returned to him, but all of this depends on him individually. Every person wants to live and this is the task that stands in front of him: to continue to live, preserve health to old age. And I have found the means to do this in Nature.

I have one advice that pertains to all, it is provided to you orally and will serve as a prophylactic to preserve you. Not even one person in our era has had the boldness to take the reins of this training in order to develop a new quality exercise and one that will provide a benefit to humanity's life. Only one person and it is our simple Russian person, Porfiri Korneevich Ivanov, who was able to win over Nature in a practical manner imposing this tempering on his body – the strength of volition. My work is not solely my idea; my body seeks a new route, and not the one that all the ancestors have traversed and lost their individual health in the process.

It was in 1933 that I encountered this concept of mine and started to engage in tempering in order to learn in Nature that a person can survive chill and not become ill. I grasped this task in order to utilize all of nature's condition and apply them to myself.

Ivanov is not hoarding his concept, he wants to distribute what he discovered to everyone. Our task is to grasp the measures that will preserve and improve the life of people, since this struggle for the prolongation of a person's years had yet been initiated. It is necessary for all people to support initiating this effort, and especially the older generation. And it is work and labor more than all else that God will provide us from Nature, but for some reason we seem to want to think and labor in a different manner. It seems no matter what we build, to what we aspire, our entire course just directs us to the grave. But another course does exist, this other route is toward life, toward health.

First: Treatment using cold water provides a great benefit. It will excite the central nervous system. You need to bathe in cold water in the morning and evening. When you rise from bed, the first thing to do is to bathe in cold water and then go to work. Do the same in the evening. This is a natural and inartificial method of self-healing and self-preservation. Water is alive and natural, and it assists in the body developing warmth within itself. This will also improve a person's mind and mental faculties.

Second: All of us are identical with respect to Nature, meaning, we have a duty to be respectful toward each other, to show courtesy to each other. When you walk along the street and encounter some strangers, or old men or women, we must greet them courteously, we have the obligation to deal politely with all people, to welcome them. What will we achieve doing this? We motivate others with our words for them to know that we have not forgotten about them; we also want them to prolong their lives. For our goodness, Nature will compensate us with its goodness. Today you will do this and tomorrow you will continue to live on this account.

Third: Due to our ignorance our life progresses unevenly among us, many seem to have this deficiency. So we see a destitute or underprivileged person off to the side. This is that person's illness, and we do not help them. We need to be aware of needy persons and extent our charity and assistance to them and without second guesses. Nature will reward in the future.

Fourth: We have accustomed ourselves to greedily eat and eat more than we should and eat better, we have accustomed ourselves to an excess of food. However Ivanov has discovered in Nature the capacity to avoid eating or drinking 42 hours each week in order to vacate the alimentary canal of its contents, and this will also provide rest for our body as a organism. The select time to perform this is from Saturday morning to Sunday afternoon. But before you sit at table to dine, go outside barefooted, and raise your head and breathe heavily in the clean air several times.

The body will absorb strength in inhaling and exhaling. The air that surrounds a person is permeated with nourishment, this ether that moves in the air and penetrates the entire human body as an organism. It likewise restores the capacity of the lungs and cleanses them. Air contains life-providing strength in the interests of a prolonged life. Water and earth: when I go outside it is always without shoes, I only wear trousers, I raise my head and as

Nature to provide me its strengths for me to receive and lead a sick-free life. The earth as you know contains a current, electricity, magnetism. The earth surrounds us with its current and so the necessity of having to walk barefooted.

Nature has taught me what I needed to do to be healthy, and not to become ill or chill. My advice is easy and useful. By taking my advice a person will have his previous health restored to him, and by applying my method of tempering the body this will serve as a prophylactic to preserve it from illness and chill.

Fifth: Do not even smoke or drink hard liquor. The harmful effects of smoking have long been proven by medicine, but the majority of people do not have the ability to mobilize their moral strength and discard this harmful habit. But I have the means of helping a person if he definitely wants to discard smoking. If he turns to me I will help him stop and it will be easy. I can also help someone discard alcohol, as long as he turns to me with his request to do so.

You, just as with all people, were born for the purpose of living, for the purpose of life, but our capricious conduct in Nature forces us to die prematurely. This is due to our ignorance of the mater, and in general we have been doing nothing over the progress of our life to acquire an easy and prolonged life. A person tempered by my method, can remain without clothing, without food and water, or even a sheltered residence, and under the worst of conditions of the elements. This is attained through the individual's compliance in my tempering, for the person to learn how to acquire these strengths from Nature, and which will then preserve the person's health in a natural manner.

We need to be one with Nature and retain an indivisible tie to it. We need to have a love toward Nature, and not one that is capricious or disdaining. We will learn from Nature to be friendly one toward another, to preserve and shelter one another, to love one another, and this will also terminate all way. This is what we will acquire from nature. Prisons and hospitals will disappear

Over the past two thousand years this has been prepared for us and now disclosed to everybody. Let Nature surround us and it will provide us life-giving strengths and will illuminate us forever and ever.

The Teacher Ivanov

August 29, 1967

PORFIRI'S PROVERBS

The hottest summer and southern [Russian] sun does not harm me and will not sunburn me.

I walked the winter in the frost and snow without clothing and shoes.

I was buried in the snow naked for half-an-hour just to test what effect it would have on me, and when they dug me up, steam was emanating from me due to the natural warmth of my body.

I can bathe in the sea and rivers in winter, and remain their for an unlimited period of time.

After a hot steam bath in a sauna, sweaty and wet, I walk without clothing in the frost and snow without clothes and barefooted, and I enjoy it even better when I wallow in the snow.

In winter with temperatures at 20 degrees below freezing point, I stood on a steamboat deck, and on another occasion I traveled bare-chested on the front of a train through several stations.

The final and supreme achievement of my endeavor with control of my body due to my tempering was the development of defensive strengths and the capacity of subjecting them to my volition, which allowed me to not only endure any elements of Nature, but also to defeat any illnesses at their onset, not only in myself, but also in other people.

My method of tempering provides not only a general tempering of the body as an organism against cold and chill, but includes stimulation and development of all latent defensive strengths, mechanisms of the body, due to which a person can endure any unpleasant exposure to the elements, without harm and even to his personal benefit, and likewise to repel and recovery from any illness.

Healing is provided relative to the amount of faith, but faith without observance is lifeless. God is the deity that does not do harm. God does not reside in heaven, but here in the world, in people who attain a victory in their life.

A characteristic mistake is the attempt to only observe part of the principles, to separate them into obligatory and convenient. This incorrect attitude particularly toward *Detka* will lead the person to not fulfilling any of them at all.

All evolves based on the laws of Nature, there is nothing outside of these laws. The human is the initial small cell that is planed by Nature on Earth.

Bathe in cold water twice a day, and it will improve your health. Bathe where you can: lake, river, bath house, either a shower or at least pouring water over yourself. Replace a hot bath with a cold.

Be cordial with everyone everywhere, especially with aged persons. Do you want to be healthy? Be healthy in the presence of others.

Become as I am: a Victor over Nature.

Childhood, adolescence, and the early adult years of my life I spent just as do other people. I was not a super-natural person and their was no morals of which I should brag about having. I was a criminal in Nature, I pillaged it, I ruined other people's happiness, I would never settle any matters with anybody, I just concentrated on building my own welfare, I did all I could for myself to live well. Then I departed from all of this, and changed course toward Nature and so become a close friend of Nature.

Children, you are full of desire to be productive to the entire Soviet nation that is building communism. To do this, aspire to be healthy.

Defeat greed, lethargy, contentment, pride, that exists within you. Believe in people and love them. Do not say anything bad about them, and do not allow dishonest opinions of them to be near your heart.

Dirt on the outside of the body is not bad. My best helper is the dirty and damp soil on the banks of rivers, it maintains healing power. The bad dirt is what is inside of us.

Do not be afraid of cold water – it is alive!

Do not be in such a hurry to live. Speed is a display of foolishness.

Do not separate intent from action. You read about it, good, but what is principle is to accomplish it.

Each person is provided the right of choice: either consciously construct yourself in a manner where Nature will help, defeating illness inside and outside of yourself, or continue to ignore what is occurring and which will inevitably lead you to ruin.

Everyone can die, we need to learn to live.

God does not reside in heaven but here on Earth, in people who were able to gain control over themselves.

Help people to the extent you can, especially the destitute, illness, oppressed, needy. Do this with happiness.

I am the same as other people, except that I possess the strengths that other people do not possess. I have the strengths of Nature: air, water and soil. I loved, do love, and will love forever all of you, my dear friends who are not capable of dying.

I ask, I beseech all people. Stand and take your place in Nature. It is not occupied presently by someone else and you will not purchase it no matter how much money you spend, but you can only acquire it through your individual effort and labor in Nature, and this will be to your benefit and life will be easier for you.

If a person lives in a manner compatible with Nature, then Nature will preserve him during any calamity or disaster.

In 1933, I encountered my concept and started to occupy myself in tempering in order to utilize all of Nature's available elements to my benefit. I took nothing from the ceiling, nothing to already dealt with national medicine. I listened to lectures on the harmful effects of tobacco and wine. My body refreshed in Nature.

It is absolutely necessary to stand barefooted or lie on the ground in the snow, as the ground will absorb illness.

Liberate your head from thoughts about illness, maladies, death. This is your victory.

This is not a normal tempering of the body as an organism against cold and chill, but a stimulation, development and conscious control using inner strengths and capacities of the nervous system.

We were born to live, but somewhere along the way we seem to be doing otherwise. We have started to descend, helplessness is now displayed in our body. We love warm weather, and reject the cold. The body has become soft. But Nature will allow us to overcome the need of clothes, but we have not learned how to defend ourselves.

Wine and tobacco destroy the human body. Whoever smokes harms his body and his heart.

You must have love for Nature, and not indifference or disdain. A person will not harm Nature, but it is Nature that has the capacity of harming a person. With reconciliation the struggle for existence between them will cease, and instead they will preserve each other.

You need to preserve your body, as it is the materialization of Nature. Energy and electricity resides in it. Nature and the person are one and the same, no difference between them.

RUSSIAN BIBLIOGRAPHY

Иванов, П. К. *Труды*

Иванов, Порфирий, и Иванов, Юрий,
Бог Родился в России, Истоки

Иванов, Порфирий, и Иванов, Юрий,
Учение, Идия

Славгородская, Лариса Николаевна,
Порфирий Иванов, Чудеса, заповеди, жизнь

PORFIRI IVANOV

Printed by BoD™in Norderstedt, Germany